ACHIEVING ACADEMIC PROMOTION

D1381362

SURVIVING AND THRIVING IN ACADEMIA

Series Editor:
Marian Mahat, University of Melbourne, Australia

Surviving and Thriving in Academia provides short, accessible books for navigating the many challenges, responsibilities and opportunities of academic careers. The series is particularly dedicated to supporting the professional journeys of early and mid-career academics and doctoral students, but will present books of use to scholars at all stages in their careers. Books within the series draw on real-life examples from international scholars, offering practical advice and a supportive and encouraging tone throughout.

Forthcoming in the series

Getting the Most Out of Your Doctorate
Edited by Mollie Dollinger, La Trobe University, Australia

ACHIEVING ACADEMIC PROMOTION

BY

MARIAN MAHAT

University of Melbourne, Australia

AND

JENNIFER TATEBE

University of Auckland, New Zealand

United Kingdom – North America – Japan – India
Malaysia – China

Emerald Publishing Limited
Howard House, Wagon Lane, Bingley BD16 1WA, UK

First edition 2019

Reprints and permissions service
Contact: permissions@emeraldinsight.com

British Library Cataloguing in Publication Data
A catalogue record for this book is available from the British
Library

ISBN: 978-1-78756-902-7 (Print)
ISBN: 978-1-78756-899-0 (Online)
ISBN: 978-1-78756-901-0 (Epub)

ISOQAR certified
Management System,
awarded to Emerald
for adherence to
Environmental
standard
ISO 14001:2004.

Certificate Number 1985
ISO 14001

INVESTOR IN PEOPLE

CONTENTS

PART II
INTERNATIONAL PERSPECTIVES ON
THE STRUCTURAL AND INSTITUTIONAL
PROCESSES OF ACADEMIC PROMOTION

ACKNOWLEDGEMENTS

We are deeply grateful to the authors of each chapter who have generously shared their knowledge of academic promotion and their personal academic career journeys. We also recognize the global network of academic colleagues whose participation in discussions, questions, and opportune comments have provided the intellectual inspiration and motivation for us to publish this work.

This book has been made possible through the support of many people. We wish to recognize the reviewers whose expertise, suggestions, and helpful critique have advanced the authors' work while also providing a global perspective to the topic of academic promotion. In particular we acknowledge Labake Fakunle and Alison Milner who took on significant reviewer roles. We also acknowledge Professor Rowena Arshad and Professor Graeme Aitken who read the full draft of the manuscript in order to skillfully draw together the main themes to open and conclude the book. Finally, a heartfelt thanks to Kim Chadwick and her team at Emerald Publishing – you have expertly guided us through the process from conception to completion with ease and the utmost professionalism.

Jennifer Tatebe and Marian Mahat

NOTES ON CONTRIBUTORS

Graeme Aitken is the former Dean of Education and Social Work at the University of Auckland, New Zealand, a position he held from July 2008 to December 2017. In his current role as a Director of Educational Initiatives, Graeme chairs the university's Academic Units and Disciplinary Area External Review panels and contributes to university teaching and learning projects.

Rowena Arshad, OBE, is Dean of the Moray House School of Education at the University of Edinburgh, UK. She is also Co-Director of the Centre for Education for Racial Equality in Scotland. Professor Arshad was awarded an OBE in 2001 for her services to race equality in Scotland. She was awarded an honorary degree by Edinburgh Napier University in 2010 for services to gender equality.

Elizabeth Balbachevsky is Associate Professor at the Department of Political Science at the University of São Paulo (USP), Brazil, Director of USP's Research Center on Public Policy Studies, and Fellow at the Laboratory of Studies in Higher Education, State University of Campinas. She is the Co-Regional Editor for Latin America of the *Encyclopaedia of International Higher Education Systems and Institutions* (Springer, 2018).

Jackie Cawkwell is an Adviser at the University of Nottingham, UK, leading on teaching and learning support staff recognition, and teaching on Postgraduate (PG) management modules. Jackie has 30 years of professional and academic experience, working in both teaching-intensive and research-focused settings. Her research interests include student transitions and academic continuing professional development (CPD).

Blair Izard is a doctoral student at the University of Connecticut, USA. She is researching the intersection of global and mathematics education. She is currently part of the Forum for International Networking in Education Leadership Team, an international group of graduate and early career researchers from U21 Schools of Education.

Jussi Kivistö is a Professor in the Faculty of Management, University of Tampere, Finland. Kivistö has over 10 years of experience in teaching, supervision, and coordination of educational programs in higher education administration and management.

Marian Mahat is a Senior Research Fellow at the University of Melbourne, Australia. Marian has more than 20 years of professional and academic experience, spanning several universities, the Australian Federal and local governments, and the private sector. Her research is focused on student learning and outcomes in different learning and teaching contexts and systems.

David M. Moss is Associate Professor at the University of Connecticut, USA, specializing in curriculum studies and internationalizing US teacher education. His current research interests are in the areas of global/international education, culturally sustaining pedagogies, and curriculum reform.

Attila Pausits is Head of the Centre for Educational Management and Higher Education Development at Danube University Krems, Austria, and Academic Director of the Erasmus Mundus Master Program "Research and Innovation in Higher Education." He has worked in many international research and developments projects related to the modernization and development of higher education.

Elias Pekkola is an acting Professor and a University Lecturer in Administrative Science and the Academic Director of Nordic joint master's degree program on Innovative Governance and Public Management at the Faculty of Management, University of Tampere, Finland.

Jennifer Tatebe is a Lecturer in the School of Critical Studies in Education, the University of Auckland, New Zealand. Her work examines the transformative potential of education in disadvantaged contexts by exploring the socioeconomic and political contexts of these educational spaces and their influence on teaching and learning.

FOREWORD

I first met Marian Mahat and Jennifer Tatebe several years ago in Chicago at the American Educational Research Association conference. Both could be described then as Early Career Researchers. What struck me then was their enthusiasm for working in higher education and their desire to support doctoral students and early career academics to find spaces to share ideas, strategies, and network. This book is therefore a natural next step to put into print some of the key takeaways from enigmatic conversations that have taken place over different years and across different continents. I wish when I started in the Academy, someone had provided me with a book like this to read.

The strength of this book is that it draws from international voices. There are chapters which are highly personal, authentic, and honest, charting the journey and lessons learnt for these individuals. These chapters provide ideas and good counsel for those wishing to navigate a route map for promotion in higher education. Other chapters provide an informative guide on how higher education institutions might approach recruitment, promotion, and progression from different country perspectives. These contextual chapters are fascinating as they largely demonstrate that there is no "one size fits all."

There are, however, some common themes emerging. The first is the importance of doing your homework. I have read hundreds of job applications and sat on many interview panels over my years in senior management in higher education. It is clear when an applicant has not prepared sufficiently. These applications look like you are recycling an application which had been prepared for another institution. No surprise then that these are quickly sifted out. Coming to interview without doing your homework of the institution you wish to join leaves a panel wondering why you bothered applying. The lack of preparation loses you traction, particularly if another candidate can demonstrate that they have gone that extra mile.

The second point is to be proactive. There will be routine aspects that a selection panel will look for such as the ability to write for publication, to write grant applications and to teach but what is more needed is for you to "stand out." The chapters in the book provide a range of suggestions such as the importance of networking internationally, taking opportunities to give talks, to use conference opportunities to look for potential collaborators, to volunteer to teach, and in general to become a good citizen and provide service. If you have a robust curriculum vitae and you have taken time to do your homework and prepare for the vacancy, those letters of recommendation (your references) are vital. You will be joining a community when you enter the Academy and many who select or promote you will not question how smart you are but they will want to know whether you work well with others and will be a collegiate member of the team. At the end of the day, do you pull together or are you likely to be a selfish academic? This book gives practical advice on how you can position yourself to get good letters of reference as well as to prepare for your promotion case.

Another theme is the ability to be flexible. Universities offer many career opportunities and it may be that your immediate chosen pathway is not available. Many of the individual stories in the book tell about the need to keep an open mind, to be creative, flexible, and to seize opportunities. The Academy is a fabulous place to be. It provides a never-ending calendar of events to stimulate your thinking, opens up a range of cultural and community offerings and where honestly, the job satisfaction is more than just the paycheck.

Mahat and Tatebe have pulled together a combination of the personal and the institutional. This book is a smorgasbord of ideas, roadmaps, and tips for those considering promotion and progression in higher education.

Professor Rowena Arshad OBE
Dean of the Moray House School of Education
University of Edinburgh

PART I

SCHOLARS' EXPERIENCES AND PERSONAL REFLECTIONS ON ACADEMIC PROMOTION

1

DEMYSTIFYING THE ACADEMIC PROMOTION PROCESS

Marian Mahat and Jennifer Tatebe

1. INTRODUCTION

One of the most important tasks for a university is capability building for the future. Academic promotion remains one of the most tangible indicators of the status of an academic. The appointment and development of successful academics and their promotion into leadership positions within the department and institution create a positive academic environment and strong departmental image.

Academic promotion is defined as a process of advancement in rank whereby a university rewards academics for their accomplishments, usually in the form of additional salary and increased roles and influence (Hardré & Cox, 2009). Put simply, it is a movement from one academic rank to a higher rank or the transition from one classification level to another. A promotion for any academic is a result of

3

demonstrated scholarly performance in teaching, research, and other criteria at the level specified within the promotion and performance assessment of each university. To be promoted, academic staff must be able to demonstrate that they satisfy the criteria for promotion by providing a cumulative body of evidence that is at a standard of performance relevant to achieving the academic level for which promotion is sought (Parker, 2008).

For the individual academic, it is important to recognize that the backbone of the academic reward system is promotion and tenure. Individuals who have chosen a career in academia need to be well informed of the sequence of promotion up the academic ladder. It is equally important to have a fundamental knowledge of specific academic career tracks, the criteria and steps required for promotion, and what tenure provides and truly means.

This chapter provides a broad overview of specific academic career tracks and pathways, and defines the process of promotion and tenure as a guideline to those who choose a career in academia. Familiarity with these issues will help aspiring academics choose an appropriate faculty position that meets their academic as well as personal goals. This chapter concludes with some tips to prepare for an academic promotion application.

2. ACADEMIC PROMOTION ACROSS GLOBAL CONTEXTS

Each chapter in this book provides a unique perspective on academic promotion from different global contexts. Tatebe provides an account of some of the opportunities and challenges moving from a fixed term contract to securing a tenure track position in the New Zealand context. Drawing on her experience as a female academic at an Australian university, Mahat reflects on her own personal journey as a female early career academic and her recent experience in applying for an academic promotion. Izard and Moss provide a compelling narrative on pursuing a tenure track faculty position in the US higher education system, viewed from the perspective of a graduate student.

Drawing on her professional experience at a UK university, Cawkwell explores the influence of external drivers on academic promotion policies and practices in the UK context. She argues that an individual academic must understand and exploit these influences in order to achieve personal success. Kivistö, Pekkola, and Pausits provide an institutional and system perspective of academic promotion in Europe, with particular focus in Finnish and Austrian higher education systems. On the other hand, Balbachevsky illustrates some of the challenges for an early career scholar navigating the academic market in Latin America. In the final chapter, Aitken offers both reflections and thought-provoking questions about the complexities of current academic promotion processes within the academy.

Acknowledging the challenge of contextual differences, this section provides a broad overview of each geographic area. While many of the academic processes are similar across contexts, the varied use of promotion terminology can make navigating the landscape confusing and bewildering. As an example, Table 1 provides the broad academic ranks that are typically used in each region. For consistency, terms such as early career academic or scholar have been used throughout the book. Early career scholar refers to academics in the first few years (between five and eight years depending on institutions) post-PhD. Acknowledging the complexities of terminology and processes across regional contexts, the recommendations provided in this chapter remain generic. Readers are strongly encouraged to familiarize themselves with the promotion application procedures of each individual institution.

2.1. North America

The academic promotion process in North American universities, particularly research-intensive ones, typically involves: a formal application, submission of a curriculum vitae, and a dossier or portfolio of supporting evidence demonstrating excellence across and within all relevant scholarly activity, and referee reports. The reference to scholarly activity is made in recognition of a growing number of universities adopting multiple academic tracks. For example, many universities offer a "traditional" research, teaching, and service track where promotion applicants must provide evidence of their engagement in research projects and corresponding publications, teaching, and relevant academic service. Some universities are adopting a "teaching" or "educational leadership" track where academic promotion criteria is more focused on teaching, involvement in the scholarship of teaching, and educational leadership and relevant academic service. A research-only track is a third, arguably less common, academic pathway. Academics in this track are more likely to be funded through research grants or philanthropic means and are often located in research centers. In this case, academic promotion criteria are more heavily weighted on research and corresponding outputs.

Table 1. Academic Ranks across Regions.

Region	Australia and New Zealand	North America	Europe	Latin America	Asia
Classification of academic titles	Level A – Tutor/ Associate Lecturer/ Research Associate	Research Associate	Assistant Lecturer		
	Level B – Lecturer/ Research Fellow	Assistant Professor	Lecturer	Asistente	Lecturers
	Level C – Senior Lecturer/Senior Research Fellow	Associate Professor	Senior Lecturer	Auxiliary/ adjunto/doutor	Assistant Professor
	Level D – Associate Professor/ Reader	Associate Professor	Associate Professor/Reader	Associado	Associate Professor
	Level E – Professor	(Full) Professor	Professor	Catedrático/ Titular	Professor

Once the relevant application documents and supporting evidence have been completed, the process of evaluating the applications may require approval from the Head of Department, review from an academic promotions committee, and approval by the Dean with the formal promotion outcome often written by the President or Vice Chancellor of the University.

2.2. Australia and New Zealand

Academic positions in Australia and New Zealand can be either continuing (permanent) or fixed-term (contract) appointments. Continuing appointments at the Lecturer level and above generally involve a three- to five-year probationary period. There are five levels of classification of academic titles of Levels A–E (see Table 1). These titles and corresponding salary levels may differ between institutions. At each level, the prospective academic must pass each university's minimum standards and promotion policies. Appointments at level A are usually for new academics, post-doctoral fellowships, and those with extensive industry experience relevant to teaching and research but who do not possess a PhD. Academics who are appointed to Levels D and E are developing (Level D) or have an outstanding (Level E) international profile and have demonstrated sustained high competence in both teaching and research. Other titles bestowed to academics may include Adjunct professor, which are honorary titles to formally recognize an academic's close association with, and significant contribution to, the academic activities of the University. Emeritus professor is a title bestowed upon a retired academic who has rendered distinguished service to the university.

Similar to the North American context, the academic promotion process in Australian and New Zealand universities typically involve a formal application, submission of a curriculum vitae, and a proposal or statement of supporting evidence demonstrating excellence across and within all relevant scholarly activity, and referee reports. For Levels D and E, referee reports usually include references from international colleagues.

2.3. Europe

While the academic promotion model in the UK is similar to the North American, Australian, and New Zealand frameworks, processes differ in different countries in Europe (see the chapters by Cawkwell and Kivistö et al). Applications involve the submission of an application form, evidence of teaching, research, leadership, and management relevant to research or teaching tracks (with some offering additional educational management tracks) a supporting letter from the Head of School (Department), curriculum vitae, and list of referee nominees. Applications tend to be submitted via University Human Resources Departments, and assessed against academic standards by an academic promotions committee. The committee recommendations are forwarded to the Academic Council with successful outcomes sent via the Head of School, College Principal or Institute Director. European universities have been proactive in developing teaching and research excellence frameworks at local and national levels. It is advisable for applicants considering academic promotion to refer to these frameworks well in advance as they can offer valuable guidance on application development.

2.4. Latin America

Academic promotion in Latin America varies between public and private universities, at Federal and State levels, and between and within countries. Balbachevsky's chapter provides a comprehensive overview of the higher education system in Latin America. Advancement is achieved through progression across levels of a given class and promotion across different classes. Each progression step normally requires two years of service plus approval in a performance evaluation, which is internal to the university. Advancement to Professor may require either a type of Habilitation (defense of an original thesis) or approval of a written document describing the applicant's professional achievements (in teaching, research, outreach, and academic administration). A committee made of at least 75% of members external to the applicant's own university usually carries out the evaluation process.

2.5. Asia

Academic staff who are interested in and with the potential for sustained excellence in both teaching and research are usually on a tenure track. Predominantly Assistant Professors are appointed on term contracts, while Associate Professors and Professors may be appointed either with tenure or on term contract (see Table 1). Education and research tracks are quite dominant in Asia. Academic staff on a research track have a focus on conducting important research of high international quality. Appointments on this track include Research Assistants, Research Fellows, Senior Research Fellows, Associate Professor (Research), and Professor (Research). On the other hand, academic staff with a focus on teaching excellence, student learning, and pedagogical research and innovation are on an Education track, and include Teaching Assistants, Instructors, Lecturers, Senior Lecturers, and Associate Professors (Educator Track). Both are normally on term contracts that are usually of one to three years. In some universities, academic staff who are scholar-practitioners with professional skills and expertise in industry to complement the teaching and research enterprise of the university are on what is called Practice track. They contribute significantly to the outreach activities of the university. Appointments are to Associate Professor (Practice) and Professor (Practice), on initial term contracts of one to three years.

3. WHAT ARE UNIVERSITIES LOOKING FOR?

Academia today has a set of promotion requirements and criteria that are different across institutions and regions, across types of roles – for example, teaching only, teaching and research, and research only roles, across grades or levels – for example, Lecturer, Senior Lecturer, Associate Professor and Professor, and discipline – some criteria are more or less relevant to certain disciplines. This would also relate to the relative emphasis given to each criterion, the relevance applicability of each criterion, and the choice of evidence that supports each criterion. However, in the main, as one progresses up the career ladder, universities are quite clear about their expectations of academic staff – one that is sometimes increasingly less about intellectual rigor but more about the bottom line – although they are not necessarily articulated in that way. As academic staff progress through the promotion levels, universities expect them to increase the quality and impact of their research outputs, as well as enhance the quality and effectiveness of their teaching and their contribution to all aspects of learning and teaching. There is an expectation that their role in the promotion of scholarship will expand and that their qualitative contribution to the discipline will increase. Among all these, they are also expected to demonstrate leadership as well as engagement and impact.

An academic promotion application usually centers around a framework that includes a number of key elements, dimensions or themes, including Research and Research Training, Education or Teaching and Learning, Engagement, Leadership and Service. One university framework may include, the three traditional core dimensions of academic performance – activity, engagement, and quality and impact – across the academic domains of Teaching and Learning, Research and Research Training, and Leadership and Service. At another university, this framework may include dimensions of Research, Education, and Engagement, with a set of criteria underpinning each.

REAL EXAMPLES OF ACADEMIC PROMOTION FRAMEWORKS

Institution A

Research

> *Research is contributing to new knowledge or using existing knowledge in new and creative ways to generate new concepts, methodologies, inventions, and understandings; communicating and disseminating that knowledge to others; sharing expertise and leading the development of staff through scholarly engagement. Research criteria include the following:*

- Advancing the discipline.

- Building reputation and recognition of research excellence.

- Quality research supervision and mentoring.

- Establishing, leading or participating in successful research teams, research units, or centers, and fostering interdisciplinary research.

- Translation, commercialization, or adoption of discoveries and policy-to-practice by external entities.

Education

> *Education is promoting effective learning and developing student potential through the creation, delivery, and evaluation of curriculum informed by pedagogy, guided by recognized standards, and enhanced by innovation and development of staff. Education covers the totality of the student experience that occurs in the educational process. Education criteria include the following:*

- Design and planning of learning activities.

- Teaching and supporting student learning.

- Assessment and giving feedback to students on their learning.

- Developing effective learning environments, student support, and guidance.

- Integration of scholarship, research and professional activities with teaching in support of student learning.

- Evaluation and development of practice leading to continual professional enhancement.

Engagement

> *Engagement is actively contributing to the governance, capacity building, and development of positive and inclusive cultures within the university, through citizenship behaviors and formal leadership roles. It also includes contributions to business, government and community organizations to the mutual benefit of all parties. Engagement criteria include the following:*

- Enhancement of the workplace and culture through active engagement and involvement in the work of the university, faculty, and school.

- Engagement with industry, government, community, and not-for-profits that contributes to positive economic, social, or cultural outcomes.

- Contributions to the advancement of the profession or practice.

Institution B

Research

> *Research activity covers all aspects of the creation and application of new knowledge, however that manifests itself within your discipline or disciplines. Broadly speaking, it covers the following:*

- The production and dissemination of research outputs, including informing policy through research insights.

- Supporting and nurturing early career researchers, including supervision of PGR students.

- Enabling and leading research activities: contributing to the intellectual life of your discipline, developing novel lines of enquiry, contributing to the development of standards within discipline, developing and maintaining cross-disciplinary research activities, contributing to addressing equality, diversity and inclusion issues in research, strategy input and reviewing for dissemination, funding and professional bodies, and generating research income at a level appropriate to the discipline.

Education

> *Education activity refers to any activities which support student learning, including the following:*

- Establishing new modules, programs and short courses.

- Developing subject materials.

- Curriculum development and learning design;

- Personal tutoring.

- Consultation and collaboration with professional bodies on course design and accreditation.

- Working with students on curriculum reform projects.

Enterprise and External Engagement

> *Enterprise and external engagement covers a wide range of predominantly externally directed activities, and, in particular, knowledge exchange activities directed at collaboration with agencies and stakeholders outside of academia, including*

*businesses and the public, to realize the impact/
benefits of research upon:*

- public discussion;

- media discussion;

- cultural life;

- quality of life;

- communities;

- equality and social justice;

- justice;

- education;

- public policy;

- commercial and social enterprise activity;

- infrastructure;

- technology and materials;

- healthcare;

- professional practice; and

- the natural environment.

Institutional Citizenship

*Institutional citizenship covers any activities,
which contribute to promoting positive collegial
behavior across a department or faculty; as well
as contributing to the effective running of the
administration and governance of the University, in*

line with the University traditions of collegiality and service. These may include the following:

- Serving on departmental, faculty or institutional committees, including selection committees.

- Involvement in, or leadership of, culture change within a discipline or department.

- Mentoring within your department or faculty.

- Advancing equality, diversity, and inclusivity for staff and students.

- Contributing to local or institutional policy development.

- Contributing to intra-departmental or cross-institution strategic activity.

- Coordinating or leading aspects of the university administrative function as they relate to a department or faculty.

Although promotion requirements and criteria may differ across institutions and regions, it is usually uniform for all academics within a single institution and may not differ from department to department. The weightings of each criteria may differ between disciplines but the requirements and guidelines are typically consistent.

4. HOW DO YOU TYPICALLY APPLY FOR AN ACADEMIC PROMOTION?

Academic promotion policies vary by context and institution. Most institutions have a formal promotion process that often includes an application and a corresponding portfolio of evidence. For many, the topic of promotion may begin well in advance of the promotion round with conversations about career pathways at annual performance appraisals and research funding reviews. If seeking promotion is on your radar within the next year, it may be valuable to initiate this conversation with your Head of Department. Informing your Head of Department of your promotion intentions serves several purposes. First, most institutions require referee reports as part of your evidence portfolio. Numerous institutions require formal support from your Head of Department. Others require additional referee reports from individuals who can speak to your teaching and research accomplishments, and your commitment to service roles at your institution and within your wider communities of practice. Part of the academic promotion process involves identifying multiple individuals who can write a comprehensive referee letter that highlights your strengths and capabilities. A second reason for approaching your Head of Department early about promotion is that it can open discussions about strengthening any gaps in experience and connect you to others who have been successful in recent promotion rounds.

5. WHAT HAPPENS IN A TYPICAL PROMOTION PROCESS?

Most institution promotion processes involve multiple stages of approval. Again, variations by context and institution are likely, so follow your promotion guidelines closely. Generally, a typical application process involves completion of an application form, Head of Department or School approval, convening of a Faculty Staffing Committee that considers all applications in accordance with the relevant guidelines and academic standards, Human Resource sign off if the application is successful, and possibly approval from the Dean or Chair of the Staffing Committee prior to notification sent to each applicant. Promotion applications may be submitted via academic or administrative channels depending on individual institution policies. Your promotion guidelines will outline the appropriate submission process. You may also be notified upon progression to each phase of the approval process or you may find you will only receive notification of the application outcome at the end of the process.

The most important part of the promotion process is the committee's review of your application. Academic promotion committees are generally composed of senior academics representing a range of expertise across the Faculty. Depending on the institution, the membership of the committee may be public knowledge. Regardless, remember that you are writing for a particular audience. They are senior scholars who have been successful at this stage in the past.

6. WHAT OTHER RESOURCES ON ACADEMIC PROMOTION SHOULD ONE BE LOOKING AT?

We recommend that you seek out as many promotion resources as possible. Actively seek out relevant institutional guidelines and frameworks from a range of sources. From the policy perspective, we suggest consulting the range of institutional policies that may include academic standards, collective agreements, Human Resources, Equity, University and Faculty strategic plans, and academic leadership frameworks. Attend all promotion workshops if available and engage with others interested in the promotion process. Working with a partner or group will keep you motivated and on task. If you know of individuals who have recently been promoted, ask if they would feel comfortable sharing their applications.

We recognize that developing a portfolio of evidence can be a big task. The good news is that you do not have to start from a blank canvas. Be strategic and draw on any previous teaching and research performance reviews. Most institutions require some form of annual appraisal so you may be able to build on previously collected evidence. Next, revise previous statements about your work for the purpose of your promotion application. Once you have completed a draft, we recommend reviewing your application with a mentor. If you do not yet have a mentor now is the time to seek someone out to help guide you. Better yet, consider approaching more than one mentor. Aim for a senior academic and then someone else who may be just ahead of you who might be able to offer more recent experience regarding promotion to the next level. If in doubt, connect with your Head of Department.

7. PREPARING FOR A PROMOTION

Success in academic promotion is marked by bureaucratic decisions and structures within universities that are guided by policies, protocols, and processes. It can be a long and tedious process but once you have made the decision to apply for a promotion – regardless of which level or grade you are applying for – here are some tips to get you promotion ready. These recommendations are intended for a broad international audience. We therefore encourage you to adapt them to your context and institution.

- *Attend the briefing.* If the university or faculty or department organizes a briefing for academic promotion,

attend it. Even if you think you know ᵕ
to know about the process, or even if you .
the previous year. Processes and criteria chang
are asked that you might never have thought of bᵕ
You might meet another colleague who is going throᵕ
the process and who is happy to bounce off ideas, read
drafts, etc. It could be the best hour you would have spent
on the application.

- *Read ALL the guidelines, website, examples, documents,
  etc. pertaining to the promotion process.* A colleague
  found out three days before the application was due that
  an external international referee was needed as part of the
  application. The instructions were buried on page five of
  a 10-page guideline document. He managed to obtain one
  but it gave him undue stress while rushing to complete the
  application on time. Another colleague realized after the
  application was submitted that the curriculum vitae was
  limited to three pages. Another did not include a one-
  page statement of achievement. Many institutions offer
  promotion guideline packages and/or workshops to help
  support promotion applicants. Obtaining and following
  any Human Resources or Academic promotion guidelines
  will provide valuable information and helpful tips and
  help set you up for success. Similarly, identifying the
  promotion timeline is critical. Some institutions only offer
  one promotion round per year, while others offer several
  promotion opportunities per annum. Promotions to
  senior academic levels such as Associate Professor, Reader,
  or Professor may have different promotion guidelines,
  criteria and timelines. Most institutions should make their
  academic promotions materials available to staff through
  internal communication platforms but if you are unsure,
  contact your Head of Department, Human Resources,

or Faculty Staffing Advisor. If in doubt, check in with a senior colleague who can point you in the right direction. Universities do need to make some of these documents more structured and coherent but it's ultimately up to applicants to read promotion documents carefully. Read all of them – it helps you manage workload, expectations, and timelines.

- *Start preparing your application early.* Regardless of context or institution, it is likely that you will be revising your promotion application numerous times. Consider it similar to writing a research grant or a publication… revision, revision, revision. Further, collecting evidence to include in your portfolio of evidence may take significant time. This may include locating and identifying evidence that you are a well-rounded academic including strong teaching evaluations, evidence of research impact, service roles in local, national and even international contexts, excerpts from teaching evaluations, research grant summary, a list of awards and prizes; and contributions to service roles at institutional, local, national, and even international levels. Once located, these pieces of supporting evidence then need to be organized and written into a coherent summary. As a busy emerging academic, time is limited so we strongly encourage each prospective promotion applicant to start preparing for promotion several months in advance of your institution's deadline.

- *Get samples of applications.* Some universities may have samples from previous applications that you can access. Review them for what was written and how it was written. Their career narrative might be different but it can help you frame your own application. If your university does not have them, ask a more senior colleague for a sample of theirs. You need to be comfortable about asking and more often than not, they are happy to help. The worse that can happen is that they say no. You move on!

- *Get a mentor.* Talking to someone who has gone through the process is gold. Talking out loud about what is going on in your head and explaining it to someone else, even if you think it does not make sense, helps you to clarify ideas and concepts. Hearing things out loud often makes them less daunting, put things in perspective and sometimes sparks new ideas. A mentor, particularly one from outside your discipline, may have points of view you had not thought of and are more objective about things. Sometimes it just helps to have someone you can have coffee with and talk things through.

- *Think about your audience.* You need to make sure that you think about the people in the promotion committee – what they might already know or not know about your discipline, your career trajectory and expertise before you begin writing. This will help you focus your ideas and present them in the most effective way. It is a good idea to assume that the promotion committee consists of people who do not know you, who are busy, reading (or even skimming) in a rush, and not predisposed to grant your promotion any consideration. Efficiency and persuasiveness will be key.

- *Consider carefully your career narrative.* A career narrative is a professional statement that describes your academic experience to date and your planned future endeavors. This statement should be a strong and persuasive case for excellence in teaching and research and make clear your valuable service contributions. As you attempt to gain experience in a number of scholarly areas, not everything you do will fit neatly into these discrete categories. You need to ensure that what looks like a disparate range of research projects, publications, and collaborations all form a coherent career narrative. You will also need to highlight your strengths while articulating the depth and breadth of knowledge that you possess. It is like writing an autobiography around a theme. The theme is important.

- *Provide evidence.* You cannot develop a career narrative based on anecdotal evidence. If you have an expertise in a particular research area, you will need to present evidence by way of publications, research grants, invitations to speak in that research space. If you have strengths in a particular skill, you will need to provide evidence of how this was put in practice. Increasingly, universities are also looking at the quality and impact of your contributions. Consider other non-traditional sources of evidence such as media mentions, presentations in public forums or professional communities of practice, etc.

- *Actively seek feedback (and give enough time to provide and respond to feedback, if required).* The applications will be reviewed by a panel so asking for assistance from a range of people will help to ensure that your application is clear and robust. Guide your colleagues – tell them what specific feedback you wish to receive. For instance, if the use of self-promotion language is challenging for you, ask your selected "critical friends" to pay particular attention to how you frame your achievements. Draw widely on your academic networks. You may consider asking a colleague in a different

Faculty or perhaps someone working in industry to review your application package. Those external to your immediate sphere of influence may offer useful suggestions on clarity of ideas and strategies from other areas of expertise. The more people you can get to read the drafts the better, particularly if they are from different academic levels and roles, as well as different disciplines. Some promotion committees have at least one person outside of your discipline. If a lay person can understand your application, there is a higher likelihood that an external committee member will understand it too. But this means that you have to be disciplined enough to have a draft of your application about two to three weeks before they are due. Do not expect people to give you feedback overnight.

8. WHAT ARE YOUR CHANCES?

Academic promotion is fundamentally based on merit so clearly demonstrating how you meet or exceed the promotion standards is key. While bias from any selection committee will always exist, focus on providing evidence that you meet the promotion standards. The selection committee is bound by many of the policies noted above which favors all applicants. If the application is unsuccessful, most institutions do offer some form of feedback and/or appeals process. Consult your promotion guidelines to find out more about these two pathways.

Does everyone have an equal chance at success? Obviously, you would need to have met the criteria for promotion. How do you assess whether you have established a strong case for promotion? The best way to do this is to check out the recent successful promotions in your faculty and then add a safety margin. For academic, legal, and equity reasons, faculties and universities are committed to being consistent in assessing academic promotion applications.

The resumes of recently promoted peers are, therefore, a good yardstick. However, you will also need to do better than your predecessors. Standards will gradually rise and you want to make sure you are not only meeting the criteria but surpassing them. The idea is to correct for the tendency to overestimate your own accomplishments.

Even when you have met the criteria for promotion, there are many reasons why academics do not apply for a promotion. You have a heavy teaching load this semester. You have to travel more this year due to fieldwork and research commitments. You have just recently got yourself into a more management role. Or maybe it is more personal. You just bought a new house. You have a recent addition to the family. Whatever the reasons are, there will always be something saying, "Wait! This isn't right! Do it later. Not now. Now is not a good time. It is just bad timing."

We suggest that you try to put any small thoughts of doubt at bay and consider applying for promotion once you meet all the relevant criteria. Your promotion application has the potential to open up academic and professional opportunities that will further enhance your career pathway(s). Also, the feedback on your promotion application may identify areas for further improvement. Regardless of the result, applying for promotion is a useful exercise in building your career narrative and building a portfolio of evidence that may be useful in other academic processes such as research evidence portfolios, applications for research and teaching awards, and annual performance reviews. In other words, your time will be well spent.

9. CONCLUSION

Applying for an academic promotion can be a daunting process. There are numerous factors to consider including: understanding your institution's policies, dedicating the time required to collect evidence and complete all necessary forms, and engaging with any pre-approval processes prior to submission. The broad aim of this chapter is to provide you with an overview of various international promotion frameworks, as well as some tips for preparing your promotion application. The rest of the book provides practical guidance and personal narratives from specific regions, countries, and situations that should help you on your journey to your next role in academia. It is hoped that this chapter and others will help demystify the process, and, as a result, sparked further thinking about your next promotion.

REFERENCES

Hardré, P., & Cox, M. (2009). Evaluating faculty work: Expectations and standards of faculty performance in research universities. *Research Papers in Education*, *24*(4), 383–419.

Parker, J. (2008). Comparing research and teaching in university promotion criteria. *Higher Education Quarterly*, *62*(3), 237–251.

2

FROM PERILOUS TO PERMANENT

Jennifer Tatebe

INTRODUCTION

Completing a PhD is a tremendous academic and personal achievement. Deciding on a career pathway afterward can be an equally challenging task. The academic job market is fraught with complexities and unknowns. There are also an increasing number of different academic pathways to choose from; however, for many, the end goal is to secure a coveted full-time academic position. In this chapter, I reflect on my post-PhD journey and my time "on the market." I explore some of the challenges and strategic considerations of a fixed-term contract as a stepping stone toward securing a tenure track position. For an increasing number of academics, my story is, or will be, a familiar one as the number of contract or adjunct jobs is on the rise. My advice for promotion from "perilous to permanent" status is driven by two questions: "what do I want?" and "what's the best use of my time?" This chapter will be of interest to an international audience including PhD candidates, early career researchers, and those going back on the job market.

CONTEXT

While this book offers an international perspective on academic promotion, my job search experience is primarily located within the New Zealand context. As such, many of the terms I use reflect New Zealand's alignment with the British academic model. The entry-level position in New Zealand is the rank of Lecturer which is comparable to an Assistant Professor in North America. Another term I will use frequently is "School" which, for many of you, will be more familiar as "Department." It may be useful to refer back to Chapter 1 for use of other internationally comparative terms. With the terminology now explained, I will begin my academic career story.

In some ways my job search experience is unique. Timing and circumstance were on my side. To set the scene, I was nearing the completion of my PhD in New Zealand and a short-term contract in my School became available. Academic positions at this time were (and continue to be) extremely limited. I was fortunate enough to secure this contract largely due to fulfilling three criteria: holding a PhD qualification, being a registered New Zealand teacher, and prior university teaching experience in the advertised disciplinary areas. I began my first six-month Lecturer contract, the same day I successfully defended my PhD.

CHALLENGES OF CONTRACT AND ADJUNCT POSITIONS

There were clearly some immediate challenges of beginning my first academic position with limited transition time from my

PhD. In my case, securing a job as the internal candidate (at the same institution where I completed my PhD) was a major advantage. Moving forward I will discuss three of the key challenges I experienced and the strategies I employed for addressing them.

Limited Preparation Time

The position I secured was slightly more focused on teaching despite being located in the "traditional" research pathway. This meant that 60% of my time was designated to teaching undergraduate and postgraduate students, 30% was for research, and the remaining 10% of my time was allocated to academic service activities. While I had just over a month's advance preparation to begin the position, I was also preparing to defend my PhD. In honor of the process, the generosity of all my participants, my time, work and energy, and the support of my supervisors, friends, and family, I made the defense my first priority. I was fortunate in that I had previously taught on some of the courses I had been assigned as a Graduate Teaching Assistant (GTA) during my PhD. For these courses, I maximized my course preparation time by reviewing previous course outlines, teaching resources, and exams. The jump from GTA to organizing a course and delivering lectures however was significant. I also initiated meetings with academic colleagues with previous experience on these courses. I sought their advice and asked if they would be willing to share their course resources. While engaging in this process I was reminded of my first year as a high school teacher furiously developing and collecting resources. One senior colleague advised me to multiply the commonly used 1:2 lecture to preparation time ratio and then double it in the first year. I am grateful to all colleagues who created a collaborative teaching space by sharing resources. Their generosity helped to make my preparation much easier and less time consuming.

In addition to being a core Lecturer, I also served as a Course Director and Administrator on three of my assigned courses. In New Zealand, this role involves curriculum development, online learning management system (CANVAS) responsibilities, general course and student administration, and leading the team of academic teaching staff. Further complicating the situation was that all three of the courses I coordinated operated across two or three campuses, each with their own idiosyncrasies and politics. I deferred back to the same successful strategy described above: I spoke with former Course Directors and Administrators. Most of them were similarly generous in sharing their experiences, and offered helpful recommendations and directed me to the appropriate person to assist with certain administrative tasks (e.g., Information Technology). From there on, it was learning by experience and finding my own leadership style. Now a four-year "veteran" in this role I've revised many of the practices I developed in my first year while also adopting a few new ones each year.

Constant Eye on "the Market"

I learned of the phrase "being on the market" from my American colleagues who, at conferences, were intently focused on this topic. In New Zealand, being on a short-term contract is code for "being on the market." As the title of the chapter suggests, I describe contract work as perilous – due to the constant awareness of my contract termination date. Reflecting back on this time in my academic career I realize that

I had two full-time jobs: my contract Lecturer position and looking for a permanent job. The most difficult part of the balancing act was time management. This process required the fulfillment of my teaching, research and service duties, and applying for academic positions across the Asia Pacific, European, and North American markets.

My epiphany came when I realized that I could do much of the preparation work well in advance of submitting my application packages. Good job applications required significant time and effort. Search committees were savvy and could easily identify generic applications. I developed my own so-called "templates" of teaching and research philosophies, as well as a very detailed portfolio of evidence of my academic accomplishments. My second revelation was that I needed to learn the language of the three geographic contexts. I engaged my contacts and networks, researched university specific promotion and tenure policies to find curriculum vitae and application templates, and then modeled my own applications on these documents. Initially, I overlooked a readily available yet invaluable resource – curriculum vitaes and online academic profiles on university webpages. Both became primary sources of institutional knowledge and exemplars of context-specific language and processes.

Eligibility and Access: Becoming Creative

The third and final challenge outlined in this chapter is the one I found the most difficult – eligibility and access to institutional funding and Professional Development (PD). In my case, the policy stipulated that contracts of less than two years were ineligible for all Faculty and university research funding and many PD opportunities. After overcoming the initial feelings of unfairness, I became creative. In anticipation of potential future eligibility, I attended research funding application workshops. I also looked for smaller funding opportunities within my School, and sought out external and philanthropic funds. While many of these creative funding sources were very small (several thousand dollars or less), they can add up. Ineligibility for funding also created the necessity for creative ways of explaining gaps in submitted funding applications and conference attendance to future search committees. I would encourage others in similar positions to do the same. Finally, I recommend considering conducting smaller scale research projects, or breaking a project into phases, or asking to contribute to a larger study within your Faculty or Research Centre in order to be research active.

OPPORTUNITIES AND INSIGHTS

Beyond the challenges of the job, my series of short-term contracts offered numerous opportunities. The next section of the chapter outlines three advantages of my "limited time" only positions that re-frame contract or adjunct work as a valuable academic career tool.

Getting "Experience"

Once I was able to look past the challenges of my short-term contract work, I was able to recognize the value of its temporary state. From this perspective, my contract was a helpful "trial" period where I was able to explore academia. One highly problematic aspect of job postings and interviews is the highly desirable quality of experience. Experience is an odd thing – you can only acquire it through having been given an opportunity to do the work. In a chicken and egg sense, most institutions seek experienced staff yet academic positions can be limited making it difficult to create a pool of desirable, experienced candidates. For this reason, contracts and adjunct positions can be helpful curriculum vitae builders. During my series of short-term contracts, I strategically sought to gain as much teaching, research and service experience as possible. For instance, to build my teaching profile I negotiated teaching on a range of undergraduate and postgraduate courses. I also served on my school's teaching and learning committee in order to maximize my time learning about teaching-related systems and processes. While I was not eligible to supervise masters and PhD candidates, I completed the mandatory postgraduate research supervision workshops so that I would be ready to take on postgraduate supervision students in the future. In sum, I regarded my contracts as opportunities to build my academic profile and gain insight into how the academy worked to prepare for future employment opportunities.

Learn to Say No

I am still learning the skill of saying "no." It's particularly difficult to say no when trying to gain full time, continuing employment. It's a balancing act where saying "yes" demonstrates being a good colleague and the willingness to contribute to the academic culture of the School. Saying "no" risks the opposite perception despite being a valid response. I discovered that some colleagues off-loaded their service or less desirable parts of the job onto new academics. At first, wanting to "fit in" and naively flattered to be asked to help organize events, chair meetings, and complete administrative tasks, I said "yes" to most of these types of requests. I quickly burned out and realized that I was doing more service and administrative work than many of my senior colleagues. Saying "no" was, and continues to be, an important time management strategy. My advice is to be strategic. Take on service roles and extra work only if it aligns with your personal and professional goals. If it doesn't contribute to your learning, say "no." Since my first contract I've added to my say "no" mantra. A mentor shared her advice for declining to take on extra work in a polite and professional manner: if interested in additional tasks, she approaches her Head of School to remove an existing service role from her list of responsibilities. This way her workload remains unchanged. This mentor employs a second ingenious strategy for declining requests to those who approach her for assistance: she asks the colleague for a direct exchange. For instance, she might say, "Yes, I can set up your course web page for you in exchange for three hours of exam marking for my undergraduate course at the end of term." She explained that most people who continually off load their work onto others are typically not interested in reciprocation. Using this "service swap" method, she avoids saying no while also making a point about academic collegiality. This example leads me nicely into the best advice I can offer – get a mentor.

Seek Advice and Get a Mentor

The phrase "you don't know what you don't know" is relevant to academic life. Learning institutional knowledge, processes, systems, and politics takes time and effort. I had to learn these aspects of the job quickly so I immediately enlisted a mentor. In fact, I sought out numerous mentors: one primary mentor, another with extensive experience and networks in schools and my field of initial teacher education, and one of my former PhD supervisors. Another benefit of selecting these three women was that it avoided overloading one person with all of my "newbie" questions. Reflecting back on my years of contract work, these women skillfully directed me to key people within the institution, introduced me to people in their local and national networks, and identified many things for me to work on that I hadn't even considered. Their generosity was phenomenal. They shared teaching resources, curriculum vitaes, current drafts of their publications, and exemplars of their study leave (sabbatical) applications. They also identified career planning tasks such as conferences, invited guest lectures, and future promotion applications that keep me informed and focused. I am deeply grateful for each of my mentors. Again, my best piece of advice is to seek out a mentor and ask for help. While I felt the need to prove myself worthy of my job, one of my mentors gave me permission to accept help when she smiled and said, "nobody can know everything." From this I learned to be a bit kinder to myself. All of my mentors are highly successful in their academic and personal lives yet they took completely different pathways. It was only near the end of my first year that I understood that my mentors had really been asking me the same question in different, subtle ways … "what do I want?"

STRATEGIC VISION – BEING "ON THE MARKET"

Document, Document, Document

The answer to the "what do I want" question was a permanent, full-time academic position. Having a clear and definitive answer allowed me to devise a strategy to reach this goal. I strongly recommend for anyone seeking to move from contract or adjunct positions to permanent and/or tenured positions to work strategically. Each month I set aside time to work on developing my teaching, research, and service profiles. For instance, I began systematically collecting evidence of my teaching capabilities which included formal teaching evaluations, emails from staff and students about my lectures, evidence of my coordination of course meetings and completion of administrative tasks, evidence of my school practicum visits, and I carefully filed away lecture slides and all teaching resources. I also had my mentors and other teaching colleagues observe and provide formal written feedback on my lectures and tutorials. These observation notes became part of my teaching portfolio. Another significant teaching-related promotion task was making constant revisions to my teaching philosophy statement that was often specifically requested in North American university job advertisements.

Begin Future Proofing

I set aside equal if not slightly more time to work on my research profile. This included writing a research statement for job applications, working on preparing research grants and funding applications (even if only to submit in the future), and of course, writing publications. A quick note to those who might be curious about preparing research grants despite being on short-term contracts. I had several strategic reasons for working on research projects and grants. First and foremost, while on contract I had access to grant writing support from our Faculty's Research Office and designated research support staff. I was also eligible for finance team support who helped to fine tune research budgets. Second, while I may not have been able to submit these developed applications, this work was evidence of being "research active." They represented my research interests and potential. I was able to draw on these research projects and grant applications in my cover letters and interviews for permanent positions. I can honestly say all search committees were impressed with this kind of forward thinking. Finally, in anticipation of securing a full-time position, I would be well placed to submit my research application soon after my employment which would be helpful in advancing my research platform.

Ask for What You Want

My final strategic vision recommendation is to *actively* tell people what you want. Following my own advice is still a work in progress. As a woman in academia I found asking for what I want to be a difficult thing to resolve. For more on this topic refer to Mahat's chapter on being female in academia. I wanted to avoid seeming "pushy" or "ungrateful" yet I also wanted to make my academic career intentions known. Ultimately, I decided to share my goal within my professional and personal networks. I began by contacting international colleagues seeking advice and asking for recommendations on available positions at their institutions. Academia is a small world. I received a lot of support and helpful suggestions of institutions to keep an eye on, and additional people to contact. This was helpful in terms of fine-tuning my templates discussed above for jobs at these particular universities and colleges. I then set up a meeting with my Head of School about my career development. At this meeting I informed her of my international job search and asked what opportunities might become available. Two positive outcomes ensued. First, she was fully supportive of my international search and offered to write reference letters to support my applications. Secondly, she indicated that some jobs might become available at our university near the end of the year. I was unaware of this possibility so it gave me hope and made me even more focused on developing my full research, teaching, and service profiles.

MAKE THE BEST USE OF YOUR TIME

Identify Your Blind Spots

With the goal of a permanent full-time position in sight, the question of "what's the best use of my time" directed my decision making. With approximately six to seven months left in my final contract I identified three priorities that nicely extend the recommendations from the previous strategic vision discussion. I decided to find my "blind spots," or areas that may be considered weaknesses in future job applications. In my case, a glaring blind spot was the absence of research supervision (master's and PhD students). As mentioned earlier, I was not eligible to take on supervisions due to my short-term contract status. Instead, I decided to ask my colleagues if I could be an advisor for any master's students they currently supervised. For a variety of reasons including timing and the nature of the projects this initiative was unsuccessful. Not to be deterred, I asked if I could examine any master's theses. I received three offers to be an examiner. This was a valuable process that is also considered to be service to the academic community. More than service it opened my eyes to the relatively short-time (one-year) time cap for writing a master's thesis. A third opportunity I initiated was to supervise a master's student from another local institution. The research lay well outside my scope of expertise in the medical sciences; however, the project required knowledge of educating patients and the public. I was able to offer support in terms of literature on pedagogy and community outreach. Writing was a third area I made significant contributions to for this student. Added benefits were learning about institutional differences and building my local university network.

Raise Your Visibility

Academics are operating within a new era where the public voice and technology are opening up new possibilities for becoming known or "raising your profile." Amidst the plethora of options from public lectures, "scholactivist" work, to leading projects in different communities of practice, and tweeting, raising your profile and visibility can be a bit overwhelming. For those on contract or adjuncts like I was I would suggest casting your net a bit wider and consider national and international platforms for your research, teaching and service. I was fortunate to continue international-level service that I began during my PhD. My university is part of the global Universitas 21 research intensive university network. At that time, I was part of a team that organized and facilitated networking events for postgraduate students at major international academic conferences. I didn't fully realize the perception of this kind of international service. I enjoyed organizing events, and had some professional experience through one of my former non-academic jobs. I didn't think about it as strategically as I should have. It was only when a very senior academic drew the parallel between our service work and running a major research center that I understood the impact of international service. My advice is to try and find ways to engage internationally as most universities are now globally focused. International service may take numerous forms from engaging in international collaborations in research or writing, research consortia, chairing conferences, and attending annual events and workshops. There are usually streams for postgraduate students and early career scholars at these types of events that often seek volunteers. Answer that call.

CONCLUSION

Moving from "perilous to permanent" can be a lonely and stressful endeavor. Throughout the chapter I have promoted the re-framing of contract and adjunct work to focus on the opportunities available during this transitionary period. Drawing on my own experience on several entry-level academic contracts I have shared my wayfinding in hopes of assisting others to work toward their academic goals. For me, achieving a full-time permanent position was accomplished through strategic thinking and actions. By the time I was at the interview stage I was able to address all research, teaching, and service questions confidently. Further, my preparation addressing my blind spots and having carefully crafted ways of signaling my interest and potential to supervise and submit research grants was well received. Now in my fourth year of my Lecturer role I am looking forward once again to the next promotion process using many of the same strategies from my "perilous" days.

3

BEING FEMALE IN ACADEMIA

Marian Mahat

INTRODUCTION

Along the corridors of the ivory tower of academia, I continue to hear whispers of "why does he get paid more when we do the same work?," "how do I balance work and family responsibilities without compromising either?," "I can't be at that meeting, conference, seminar, dinner, drinks [insert one], sorry." Although the gap is getting smaller, the proportion of female academic staff in Australian universities is still less than 50% and only 30% of Professors (Level E) and Associate Professors (Level D) are women (Universities Australia, 2017). After years of promoting gender equality and diversity, women in academia are still failing to break through the glass ceiling.

In a world where some (predominantly male) colleagues gets undue credit and airtime in academia and some women struggle to juggle work and family responsibilities, this chapter provides some reflections about my own personal journey as a female early career academic, as well as my recent experience in applying for an academic promotion. Appended within this chapter are also some advice and tips from other female colleagues who have recently been successful in their applications for promotion. I am only a drop in the ocean of academia but hopefully these reflections will help other female colleagues who are trying to navigate the academic world.

MY PERSONAL JOURNEY

At a recent International Women's Day, a colleague said in a presentation, that every person's journey is different. My journey is different from yours and yours will be different from others. It is how you travel on that journey that is important. I can't tell you my academic journey without relating it to some personal events that happened along the way. It's only meant to set the context and highlight some of the challenges and opportunities of being female in a male-dominated academic world.

I have worked in the higher education sector for almost 20 years. I started as an entry level administrator while completing my master's. Very early on, I was interested in doing research and enrolled in a PhD part-time upon completion of my master's. This I undertook while working full-time and at the same time, advancing into more senior management roles. I also did some research assistance work, amidst all this. After about 10 years, I left a policy advisory role in institutional planning, which supports and contributes to strategic decision making by the University's senior executive group.

I moved interstate to support my partner's career at that time, and became a stay-at-home-mum to look after two beautiful children. I also withdrew from my doctorate to focus on my family. Three years on, I decided to re-join the workforce and worked in the local state government in a strategic and business development role. After only a month, my partner was headhunted back to Melbourne. I started a role in a newly developed Federal government office, which governs the quality of the tertiary education sector in Australia. In this role, I provided strategic and policy advice on the quality of higher education at both system and institutional levels. I prepared high-level proposals and briefings to the Commissioners and the Minister of Education at the time. I also prepared briefings for Senate and responses to Questions on Notice asked by Members of the Legislative Council to Ministers.

I started re-connecting with colleagues in the higher education sector through my work in the Federal government. This re-kindled my interest in pursuing a doctorate although I felt that it was a bit late in my career to pursue a PhD. I had a young family, a mortgage – I was convinced that if I wanted to go down this path, I was going to do it fulltime. After much deliberation, I left my government job a year later, secured a double scholarship and enrolled in a PhD at the University of Melbourne.

In my previous doctorate experience, I felt isolated and alone. This time round, I was adamant that I was going to make the most out of my PhD life. In the first year, I did some tutoring and lecturing while trying to refine my research questions for my doctorate research. It was around this time too that my marriage started to break down. My partner and I moved out of our marital home at the end of my first candidature year. In the second year, I secured a Research

Fellow role – as a researcher as well as a project manager, managing several externally funded research projects. During this time, I also volunteered to take on various tasks within the department – organizing seminars, developing and re-designing curricula, writing grant proposals, among other things. I also undertook some external paid consultancy work. In my final year, I was resolute that I needed to focus on writing my thesis. I cut down on paid work and enlisted familial help to look after the kids. At around this time, I started thinking of life post-PhD. Did I want to pursue a career in academia? With my experience in professional and policy roles in higher education, did I want to pursue a management focused role instead? I started perusing recruitment and universities' Human Resource (HR) websites looking for potential jobs.

I submitted a draft of my thesis to my supervisors two and a half years after I started my candidature, went on a month-long trip across Europe to present my research findings at academic conferences, and came back to respond to my supervisors' feedback on my draft thesis. I also started submitting job applications – casting my net as wide as possible while trying to stay geographically local. Life, however, has a funny way of twisting things. As fate would have it, mum, who lives overseas, was admitted into hospital for reasons unknown. I was fraught, tests were being conducted. I spoke to specialists here and overseas to get second and third opinions, anxiety ran high. The day after I presented my research at my completion seminar (a public presentation of my research findings prior to submitting the thesis for examination), I flew overseas with my two children to be with mum.

In between hospital visits and spending time with mum and looking after two children, I finalized my thesis. I submitted my thesis on my official "submission date," some 6,000 km away from my institution, exactly three years after I started my PhD journey. It was very uneventful. I remembered sitting at the dinner table, having just pressed the submit button, thinking, "Where was the applause, the fireworks, the accolade?"

I came back to Melbourne two months later, not knowing what I was going to do for a job post-PhD. My scholarship monies had stopped the minute I submitted my thesis and I was getting anxious. By this time, I was convinced that I wanted a job in academia. But the pickings were slim. I submitted more job applications and sent expressions of interests (unsolicited emails) to university departments that were doing interesting work. Some responded, some didn't. Coffees were had, but nothing really eventuated.

It was also around this time that I experienced bullying at the workplace. I referred to policies at the university, spoke to a range of people including those in HR and Ethics Integrity Unit. I weighed my options in terms of my possible courses of actions – thinking about future employment opportunities but mostly what it would mean to me personally and my family. In the end, I opted for the easy way out and decided to resign from my current role. Being a female in academia had some bearings on my decision at the time.

Three months of long sleepless nights later, I secured a job in a research-only role for a large Australian Research Council linkage project. Not long after that, I received news that my PhD examination was completed and without further examination or amendment required. Both happened in quick succession and were the best things that had happened to me in a while. I was stoked.

APPLYING FOR A PROMOTION

Most academics have a role which combines research, teaching, and administrative responsibilities. The balance of time spent

on each of these roles can vary widely according to the time
in the academic year, your experience and any administrative
responsibilities you take on. Research-only (and teaching-only)
roles are quite common in academia, but the vast majority are
appointed on a fixed-term basis. Being in a research-only role
meant that I could focus on research and publication activities,
a key measure of success in advancing in academia. For the next
months in my new role, I immersed myself in research activities for the project. This was, in addition, to writing academic
publications from my PhD research, writing grant proposals
and being involved in other smaller projects. Because I was on
"soft money," that is, fully research funded, these "additional"
activities tended to push to the margins of my "normal" working life and were performed without pay.

About eight months into my new role, I attended a briefing
for academic promotion held by the university. At the time, I
had no intention of applying but I wanted to prepare myself
for the eventuality. Hearing some of the questions being asked
at the briefing, I realized that I was probably more "qualified"
to apply for a promotion than some others. At the briefing,
I met some very senior academics and spoke to them about
how I should start building my career narrative. One offered
to read my Curriculum Vitae (CV). The response I received
after sending my CV was, "You're possibly not quite there
yet." Another senior academic I met on a different occasion
also commented about the whole promotion process; how
time consuming it was, how fraught with tension it was – the
basic premise being that one should not put oneself through
it. As a side note and probably not related (I let you be the
judge of it), both were men.

I read and re-read the criteria for promotion. And no matter how I viewed it, I was quite sure I met all the criteria and
even surpassed them. However, I just started my new job, and
I felt that I should focus on settling into my busy but exciting

new role. After much deliberation, I made the very difficult decision to submit an expression of interest to apply for the promotion. My decision was based on two main factors: one, I was never going to be less busy in the future. And two, I was convinced that I was not going to get the promotion on my first try anyway so I should go through the experience of putting together the application for future attempts.

It took two months from the time I expressed my interest to submitting the final application. During that time, I spoke to two female academics who were successful in their promotion applications in the previous year. My supervisor provided some excellent advice and was the first person to send me a sample of his application proposal. I also consulted the librarians who helped me articulate some of my research outputs. I spoke to a few other close colleagues about how best to develop my career narrative.

I was advised by a senior male academic to check the "Performance relative to opportunity" box and to provide details of how my academic performance might have been impacted by life experiences such as taking time off work to have children. In a career that requires self-confidence and resilience, particularly when applying for promotion, this advice undermined my self-esteem. I started questioning my achievements and triumphs. I wanted my promotion application to be assessed based on merit – not on some criteria that belittles the academic contributions made by women in academia. As it is, there are already many challenges faced by female academics. After nights of reflections, I checked the box anyway because I realized it was not a "checkbox" *just* for women. Male academics do this too. In my commentary, I phrased my "performance relative to opportunity" in a way that would reflect my strengths rather than my supposedly "secondary" performance.

About a month before the application was due, I sent my draft proposals to several colleagues who provided advice and feedback on a range of matters. Some provided substantive advice, others proofread and a few others provided moral support. I went through a few HR hiccups (be prepared for hiccups) but otherwise, the process of submission was quite straightforward. I submitted the application and forgot about it (for the most part anyway).

To cut a long story short, I found out five months later that I was successful in the application for promotion. I was one of only three people who was successful that year in my Faculty at every level. Perhaps not many applied but it made me feel good anyway. As most women do, I underestimated myself and the contributions I have made to academia. However, my happiness was short-lived. Being on "soft money" and in a multidisciplinary research project, the issue of who should contribute monetarily came up. The lack of policy around it meant that there were no clear guidelines. And the University's bureaucratic infrastructure meant that papers just get shuffled around, perhaps in the hopes that things will resolve itself. The promotion is in hand but the matter of funding is still up in the air ... my journey continues.

LESSONS I LEARNT

Being female in academia brings challenges but some of my experiences are not limited to being a female academic – it can happen to anyone. This is, however, my story. Thus far. And regardless of the result of my academic promotion funding and regardless of where this brings me, I learnt through this process, that I should keep myself grounded at all times. Having gone through the academic promotion process, here are some of the lessons I learnt that could potentially help others in their journey for academic promotion.

- *Focus on strengths rather than weaknesses.* Within my promotion proposal, I started sentences with "I achieved these extraordinary outputs while …," "I was able to … during which I also …." I found that shifting my focus from weaknesses to strengths instilled confidence and positivity which came through in the application. List out the reasons, facts, and opportunities – things that made you successful. This is what can differentiate you from other candidates.

- *Keep a record of achievements.* I found out too late that I should document and keep a record of my achievements. Because I wasn't planning to apply for a promotion at the time, my records were sporadic and kept in many different forms. Start a system and be consistent. As a graduate researcher or early career academic, you might think that you don't have much to start with so you'll do this later when you are a bit more established. Trust me, you'll thank yourself later.

> *Early in my career it was suggested to me that I document everything I do in my work from those smaller achievements like organising a seminar with a visiting academic to those more obvious big achievements such as being successful with a grant application. This can be a useful trigger for when it comes to writing a promotion application and can provide nice examples of success. It was also great to have a support network of trusted colleagues that were willing to share their promotion applications with me and provide feedback on my application.*
>
> *Dr Victoria Millar,*
> *Senior Lecturer*
> *The University of*
> *Melbourne*

- *You need to not only reflect on your past achievements but on also your future aspirations.* I read on a website once that particularly in the early stages of one's career, your value in the career market is almost completely based on your potential. This has stayed with me in every job application and interview. If you are applying for a promotion, you are more than likely to have met the criteria for promotion, so it is equally important to articulate clearly the value you can provide to your university and faculty. What do you have now that can help you build skills, gain exposure, and fill in gaps in your knowledge that are valued and consistent to the university's and faculty's core agenda.

- *Believe in yourself.* Most women tend to undervalue themselves. A senior female academic once said that women might meet three of the five criteria and think they are *not* appropriate/ready for the role. However, a male academic might meet two of the five criteria and think he is over qualified. Sometimes you are ready before you think you are.

- *Self-reflection of our own character and achievements is not a normal human activity, more so for women.* There must be

Going for promotion was not on my radar – I didn't think I was ready, and quite frankly, I didn't want to put in the huge effort it takes to write a promotion application until I thought I had a good chance. It took strong persuasion from colleagues outside my department for me to apply.

Writing the promotion application itself was painful because essentially, you're being asked to "toot your own horn" and write (a lot!) about how great you are, as well as how you've been recognised both nationally and internationally for your great work. It's quite an excruciatingly awkward and uncomfortable process. But one of my colleagues advised me to write it like I was writing about someone else, and that advice helped.

Dr Chi Baik, Associate Professor in Higher Education, The University of Melbourne

something in our genetics that make women less able to

"sell" ourselves. But there is also a bigger issue here. I once overheard a conversation between two women at a university café, "When he used the word 'we' to flag the department's accomplishments, he was applauded for it – for showing great leadership. When we do it, the accolade actually goes to the team, not us. If we say 'I', then we're selfish and only seeking the glory for ourselves. We can never win." There are two lessons to be learnt here. First, you *need* to sell yourself. Write about yourself like you're writing a reference for someone. Then replace the words he/she to I. Second, if we continue to think of women as "less capable," we will perpetuate that culture and thinking. We have to change our mindsets within us before we can change the mindsets of others. Start within you.

- *Find someone you can trust as a mentor or better still develop a peer-support group.* When I first started my academic career, I asked a senior female academic whether she would be my mentor. Her response was "Did someone put you up to this?." I was perplexed and obviously let down. She realized I wasn't joking, tried to make amends and offered to have coffee with me. Nothing eventuated out of it. I was disillusioned. I realized that the idea of "women sticking together"

> *Looking back at the promotion process, what I found most helpful to me was to have a mentor and supervisor who is supportive of my promotion application and recognises that it is important that my work and achievements be acknowledged and celebrated. It can feel too self-serving to initiate your own promotion so having someone who can advocate for you on your behalf makes the process feels more purposeful and less daunting.*
>
> *Dr Esther Chan,*
> *Research Fellow*
> *The University of*
> *Melbourne*

does not necessarily sit well in academia. In the end, I started an informal group of graduate researchers and early career academics. We met for a drink every month to talk about work and life. The group has grown from strength to strength. Coming into its third year now, we still meet once a month. I usually invite a successful and established female academic to join us and we usually have an informal discussion around a theme over a drink or two. It has been an extraordinary forum. We are free to voice our thoughts without being judged, and having like-minded people around you going through the same thing – sharing information and solutions to common situations – makes you feel that you are not alone.

- *Be grateful and express it.* It is sometimes hard, especially in difficult times, to see what there is to be grateful for. Even in the toughest times, there are many reasons to be grateful. Every now and then, it doesn't hurt to take stock of just how good you have it. And say thank you. When I wrote the proposal for academic promotion, I realized that the many achievements I had would not have been possible without the support of many wonderful people – professionally and personally. I took time, following the submission of my application, to be grateful and say thanks to people around me. For without them, I wouldn't be where I am today.

There are many deeper societal and economic issues related to being female in academia. Issues that I have not even touched but have graced many headlines around the world and are still current and common. The fact that we have an International Women's Day says it all. Stereotypes of women abound in academia, and often these stereotypes are subtly expressed and shared by other women as much as men. If we are to create spaces in academia where we have diverse colleagues and flexible working environments, we have to start within ourselves. What that is I can't quite articulate, yet. I will, however, leave you with this quote for self-reflection, "Talent is God-given; be humble. Fame is man-given; be grateful. Conceit is self-given; be careful" – John Wooden.

ACKNOWLEDGMENTS

I am most grateful for the insightful contributions of Drs Chi Baik, Esther Chan, and Victoria Millar. My thanks also go to the Women in Higher Education group for their support, continued friendship, and camaraderie.

REFERENCE

Universities Australia. (2017). *2016 Selected inter-institutional gender equity statistics*. Canberra, Australia: Universities Australia. Retrieved from https://www.universitiesaustralia. edu.au/uni-participation-quality/Equity-and-Participation/ Women-in-universities/Selected-Inter-Institutional#. WvzIMEiFPD5

4

RAISING THE BAR: LANDING YOUR FIRST ACADEMIC POSITION IN US HIGHER EDUCATION

Blair Izard and David M. Moss

INTRODUCTION

This chapter will unfold in four distinct sections designed to help early career scholars gain valuable insight into the complexities of preparing for and succeeding as a faculty member in the United States' (US) system of higher education. In the following section you will learn a bit about the vast and multifaceted landscape of higher education across the US. We recognize the enormity of such a task within the limits of a single book chapter such as this, and thus hope you are inspired to seek more regionally and institutionally specific perspectives as appropriate to your own interests. The second section offers a narrative from the perspective of a doctoral candidate working strategically to help ensure a smooth transition to a faculty appointment in the US system. In this section you will get some perspective on doctoral programs in the US and the day-to-day work of a doctoral candidate. In the following section of this chapter we offer advice for engaging in impactful and innovative work to help ensure your early career success. Finally, we present brief perspectives from several colleagues who remind us of the larger picture of what it means to truly thrive in the competitive environment of higher education.

THE CONTEXT OF HIGHER EDUCATION ACROSS THE US

Institutions of higher education (IHEs) across the US are as varied and complex as the cultural regions in which they reside. There is even remarkable variability within institutional designations, and terms such as "college" and "university" are grounded within both historical and institutional contexts, surprisingly without a standardized set of criteria. Although the norms and traditions of post-secondary education in the US may present as an unsolvable puzzle, with a few cultural and organizational clues, an early career scholar can make sense of this sometimes-overwhelming complexity and learn to thrive within the robust academic community, that is, the US system of higher education.

Let's begin with the notion of institutional mission and classification. With regard to colleges and universities, institutional mission sets the tone for the nature of faculty appointments and ultimately student experiences. Although institutional mission is often thought of along a continuum of research-intensive schools to those that are more teaching focused, in the twenty-first century, that bimodal distinction between research and teaching is in many ways a false dichotomy. Although many IHEs may have at one time focused on teaching *or* research, faculty at most four-year institutions are now expected to engage in a broad range of scholarly activities and teaching. As will be addressed later in this section, the nature of those activities may vary considerably across institutions. If you are interested in a predominantly teaching position as your primary professional activity, the community colleges (leading to an associate's degree) across the US represent a network of thriving IHEs and a viable option for many individuals. The balance of this chapter, however, will focus on four-year IHEs and our discussion will be geared toward tenure eligible, commonly known as tenure track, faculty appointments.

Perhaps this continuum characterizing university scope and mission can be best understood by considering the designated classifications of IHEs. The standard for classifying post-secondary institutions in the US is the Carnegie Classification of Institutions of Higher Education (see http://carnegieclassifications.iu.edu/). Using a methodology to categorize research activity, the nature and number of degrees granted (doctoral, masters, baccalaureate, and associates), along with a host of other parameters, schools are afforded a designation which best reflects the institutional characteristics and mission. For example, at the University of Connecticut (the authors' home institution) we are designated, among other labels, a public, four-year highly residential, doctoral university with the highest research activity. Although there is considerable variability even with institutions with similar classifications, it at least sets the tone of what an early career scholar might expect with regard to the nature of a faculty appointment in terms of how much effort one would be expected to allocate toward research, teaching, and service. In contrast, at what are commonly known as liberal arts IHEs in the US, there is typically a strong emphasis on undergraduate education at these smaller colleges. At the University of Connecticut, there are approximately 32,000 students (both undergraduate and graduate), which could represent a tenfold or more increase over the number of students at liberal arts colleges. Yet, such an undergraduate focus at liberal arts colleges does not preclude an expectation of a robust scholarly agenda. As mentioned earlier, the nature of professional activities may vary considerably both across and within IHEs, so let's take a closer look at the nature of faculty appointments.

A focus on acquiring external funding for research, publications (articles, books, media, etc.), service to the university and profession, and other parameters may differ with institutional focus – and understanding those norms is key to the success of an early career scholar. It is important to recognize that we are discussing in the broadest possible terms these faculty expectations, and ultimately one must come to understand the norms at the local level (department and/or program) to make an informed decision regarding fit. This notion of "fit" is critically important for early career scholars and is essential to initiating a successful career. We'd like to briefly elaborate on the expectations for research, teaching, and service as they are central for considering the notion of fit between you and a prospective IHE.

For faculty across the US, service is a fundamental element of faculty work as, to various degrees, university faculty are engaged in a model of self-governance. That is, faculty have significant participatory responsibilities regarding virtually all aspects of the academic curriculum, and collaborative committee work is the common means for faculty to address the many aspects of program creation, development, admission, and assessment. Beyond the core academic curriculum, faculty may also engage in service to the university on committees that deal with everything from library resource acquisitions to sports program compliance. Additionally, faculty members are expected to engage in service with communities, governments, and other organizations outside the university that may benefit from their expertise. Taken together, faculty service may be a considerable allocation of one's time as faculty engagement in university affairs is essential for a thriving institution.

Perhaps the most important element for ensuring success as an early career scholar revolves around an understanding of the nature and expectations for teaching and research. For most of us, we pursued this line of professional work because we bring a passion and genuine intellectual curiosity to our chosen field. One must endeavor to never lose sight of this perspective as that enthusiasm and commitment is perhaps our best way to ensure we are engaged in effort that we deem important. Teaching responsibilities will vary in terms of both levels (undergraduate vs graduate), class size, and a host of other parameters, but fundamentally also varies in terms of what is known as teaching load. That is, the number of courses one teaches in a given term and/or academic year. At one end of the institutional mission continuum, faculty at teaching intensive institutions may teach upwards of four courses per term (eight or more courses per year) and at the other end perhaps as few as one or two classes per year. Load will vary considerably by department size, enrolment, and program particulars, but one's research expectations are typically the most significant determinant of teaching load. However, it is critical not to view teaching as in opposition to research. Teaching is an essential element of the core mission of any IHE and should not be thought of as merely drawing resources from service and/or research commitments. Ideally, there exists synergy between all aspects of faculty effort.

Beyond teaching and service, understanding research expectations for faculty is essential for any early career scholar. As noted, high expectations in this regard will impact teaching load and, in some cases, with funding from external grants, one might even have little or no teaching responsibilities as funds from a grant may be used to "buy out" faculty time and hire individuals to teach classes that would have typically been assigned. At the early career stage, such a focus on scholarship may be beneficial to building an important line of research and gaining some momentum on productivity. Although the focus for graduate candidates and new faculty often center around the number of publications as a measure of productivity, given institutional mission as discussed earlier, one should not be focused merely on the volume of one's publications but on the nature and impact of one's work. Journal articles, books and chapters, creative work, technical reports, and such might be valued differently at different institutions, and early career scholars should know what is expected in terms of productivity *and* impact for their continued appointment. Thus, as an early career scholar, the notion of balance is important with regard to research, teaching, and service as engaged work across these areas will lead to impactful and engaged outcomes.

So, how does one prepare to engage in impactful research, teaching, and service? In the next section, we will highlight perspectives and priorities of the lead author of this chapter who is living this reality as a doctoral candidate pursuing work as a mathematics teacher educator with a global lens.

GETTING PREPARED FOR A FACULTY JOB

In the US, as in other countries, there is a great deal of pressure on mathematics teachers to ensure their students perform well on standardized and benchmark tests. In my secondary school teaching career, I experienced first-hand how this created a high stress environment in which teachers routinely taught to the test – focusing on the performance of mathematical procedures and the correct manipulation of numbers. I wondered what the long-term impact of such an experience would have on a generation of students who did not see mathematics as a way of understanding their world but merely as a series of numerical procedures disconnected from their lives and experiences.

As such, as a mathematics teacher, I was constantly exploring ways to teach mathematics contextually, looking to connect it to important issues of our time. As discussed in a recently published article, "Building Upon What We Already Do: Teaching Human Rights in Math", I had a vision of a classroom that realized the potential for mathematics to be used as an instrument to understand the world (Izard, 2018). Guiding questions to promote such contextual work included: "What is it like to live on minimum wage? How is wealth distributed throughout the country or world? When will a country first experience a shortage of food?" (Izard, 2018, page 114). I believe that mathematics education has the power to help students gain an understanding of their lives and society and see mathematics as a resource for making the world more equitable (Gutstein & Peterson, 2006), and I felt, as a field, we were very far from achieving that.

This sets the stage for my early career work in higher education as a second-year doctoral candidate at the University of Connecticut exploring the intersection of mathematics education and global education. I chose to focus on global education because I believe that cross-cultural international experiences for teachers shape the way they think about themselves and the world, which in turn affects their teaching. I decided to pursue a PhD in order to really dig into this work, and after completing my degree, I anticipate seeking a faculty position at a university. Following, I will provide generalized information about doctoral education in the US and share advice on how to prepare for a faculty job in the states. My current academic plan has me on-track to complete my degree in four years, so I will describe the key elements of my four-year plan.

In contrast to many countries, you're not expected to enter a doctoral program with a fully conceptualized focus for your dissertation. Instead, it's common to begin with some ideas and interests for research and spend the first two years enrolled in classes while refining your scholarly focus. Doctoral candidates in my field take about 90 credits beyond the baccalaureate degree and will typically take courses on qualitative and quantitative methods, along with other topics that build to their disciplinary knowledge base. For example, I have taken classes on research in mathematics education, grant writing, and human rights education.

Additionally, many candidates are awarded a graduate assistant (GA) position, which typically covers tuition costs and provides a small living stipend. GA responsibilities vary but often require a doctoral student to work as a research assistant with an existing faculty member and/or teach courses at the university. A full-time GA position is 20 hours of work per week, but half-time positions are also common. Half-time GA positions are 10 hours per week, and usually provide a full tuition waiver and pay half of the living stipend. Twenty hours is considered "full time" to allow for substantial effort on one's studies.

The intermediate phase between course work and dissertation varies considerably across institutions, but typically involves a comprehensive or qualifying exam and the development and defence of a dissertation proposal. The exam may be summative in nature and/or be a more purposeful bridge to dissertation by including requirements that directly support a literature review and lead to the eventual publication of one's work.

Now, here's the thing that often goes unstated – in order to be qualified for a faculty position, you need to do *more* than take courses, fulfil your GA requirements, and complete a dissertation. You should be purposefully engaging in work that will set you up for a seamless transition into a faculty role. The type of experiences you should hope to gain includes the following:

- Developing scholarly work for publication.

- Working to submit and administer grants.

- Presenting at conferences.

- Teaching courses.

- Fully participating in various aspects of university life and governance such as serving on committees.

- Networking within your field.

Balancing these demands can be very challenging. In my experience, the following strategies have proved to be helpful in maximizing my chances for success in all of these areas.

Think Like You're Bowling

To be as efficient as possible, pursuing one's doctoral studies can be a little like the game of bowling in the US – knocking down as many pins as possible with one throw helps you win the game. This metaphor comes to mind when I think about how to thrive as a doctoral student. Getting everything done would be nearly impossible if I didn't find ways to be resourceful and efficient while aligning and connecting all aspects of my professional work. For every project I complete, I carefully consider how to extend it to other areas of my academic life.

For example, many classes offer some choice in the larger assignments. Each semester, I mindfully consider my larger professional goals and consider in what ways I can leverage various assignments. Do I want to write a paper that I could turn into a conference presentation and/or publication? How can I advance my own research interests through an assignment? Can I develop the core of a grant proposal and use it apply for a grant at a later time? Can I initiate the early stages of my dissertation proposal? As a direct result of this strategic planning, I have indeed turned class projects into publications, presentations, grant proposals, and the beginning stages of my dissertation proposal. Additionally, sometimes professors will offer choice in various reading assignments, so I always use that as an opportunity to read something aligned with my interests that furthers my understandings and perspectives in my field.

Prior to considering leveraging specific assignments, I've also carefully chosen courses that expand the depth and breadth of my knowledge base. For example, I have an interest in both quantitative and qualitative research, so I've taken several classes supporting each methodological approach. Focus is also important, and my work is concentrated on mathematics education, so whenever there's a mathematics education doctoral course, I've made certain that I enrol. I'm also keenly interested in how to infuse human rights and social justice into mathematics, and as a result I've taken human rights education classes as well.

Lastly, a common bit of advice states that you can get at least two publications from your dissertation. I'm not at this point yet, but I plan to have more than a single early career publication through the work from my dissertation. All of these tips may seem straightforward, but with a long list of goals for my time as a doctoral student, it would be difficult to succeed if I didn't find ways to overlap my effort. Thoughtful planning related to knocking as many pins down as possible, with one bowling ball, is well worth the time. It will advance your work and certainly save you some time in the long run.

Pursue Your Interests

The long days, heavy workload, and seemingly endless list of things to do would be arduous if you're not interested in and passionate about what you're doing. *Motivation is key.* Establish who you are, what your near and long-term scholarly interests are and think across the framework of research, teaching, and service. Only then can you generate and execute a strategic vision as an early career scholar. Consider the following guiding questions: What are your core interests? What can you engage in immediately that will set you up for success in the future? How will you know if you are achieving your goals? Mindfully pursuing your passions will help make everything feel worthwhile and set you up for future success.

I know that I want to be a mathematics educator and work within international programs for teachers, specifically pre-service mathematics teachers. Therefore, I have been pursuing work that I'm interested in that aligns with mathematics education and global education. Here are some of the opportunities I've sought out that align with my interests:

- *Global education committee:* I am the graduate student representative on the school of education global education committee. This self-governance committee ensures the school is working toward its global education goals. For example, as committee members we consider new education abroad program proposals, and as such I have insight into the program development and approval processes.

- *Forum for International Networking in Education (FINE):* I applied and was accepted to be on the leadership team for this international organization, along with two other doctoral candidates and two early career scholars, all from various Universitas 21 (U21) member institutions. Together, we plan networking events at conferences so doctoral candidates and early career scholars can interact across a variety of professional contexts. We've also found ways to work toward our goals of disseminating our scholarly work by collaborating on research and participating together on panels and symposiums at conferences.

- *Co-teaching an elementary mathematics methods course:* I reached out to the instructor for the elementary mathematics methods course and expressed my interest in learning from her class. Together, we decided it would be beneficial for both of us to have me co-teach the course with her. This was a tremendous learning experience for me and gave me a valuable opportunity to teach a core course in our teacher education program.

See What Comes Up and Be Ready to Say Yes

Once you have established an early idea of your professional identity and the kind of work you want to engage in, individuals at your university will come to know what you have to offer. Don't be surprised if opportunities arise and be ready to say yes if it's something that makes sense for you. Because I have positioned myself as someone who works within mathematics and global education, various unexpected opportunities have come up in both areas. Here are some of the projects I've become involved with because I was ready to say yes at just the right time.

- *Nottingham Mathematics Program:* at the University of Connecticut, there are several opportunities for pre-service teachers to participate in international teaching programs abroad. We have both short term (two- to six-week summer programs), and long-term (full 15-week semester programs) options for our students. The explicit intent of these cultural immersion professional experiences is to promote students' development along a continuum from ethnocentric to an ethnorelative worldview as they develop global competences as beginning educators (Moss, Barry, & MacCleoud, 2018). In the spring of 2017, the secondary mathematics advisor in the school of education decided she wanted her students to have an option for a semester abroad experience, so she collaborated with the University of Nottingham, UK to develop the Nottingham Mathematics Program – a program that affords pre-service mathematics teachers the opportunity to engage in academic work and a teaching internship for the fall semester of their master's year as an element of their initial teacher certification program. They take classes at the University of Nottingham, intern in schools and at the world-renowned Centre for Research in Mathematics Education and immerse themselves in the British culture. They also complete what is designated an "inquiry project" – a piece of original research that is designed to help students see and consider deeper issues of schools and schooling. The program ran for the first time in the fall of 2017, and it was a huge success. We are currently planning for the next cohort of students to travel there. My role has been as an instructor and school supervisor; and I have taken on some program coordination responsibilities as well. Being in the right place at the right time and being ready to jump into this project has given me the opportunity to directly work in an international setting supporting my research interests.

- *Teaching courses:* when people know your work and interests, as well as value your level of engagement, they will be more likely reach out to you if there is a need in some aspect of the university that aligns with your work. This has been the case for me with teaching courses. As described above, I was asked to teach courses relating to the program in Nottingham, but I have also been asked to teach courses for faculty members going on sabbatical. Being willing to engage in these opportunities has given me great learning experiences and has helped both in the near and long-term with regard to my professional preparation as a developing faculty member.

- *U21 research grant project*: one day, during the FINE leadership team meeting, we started talking about how we could use our work (organizing networking events for doctoral candidates and early career scholars) to gather and report on data that could benefit the field. Eventually, we decided to form a team of four doctoral candidates from different U21 universities – University of Connecticut, University of Nottingham, University of Melbourne, and University of Edinburgh – and apply for a small research grant from the U21 organization in order to conduct research on doctoral candidates' perceptions of networking. I agreed to represent the University of Connecticut. We ended up receiving the grant and are now in the process of carrying out an original research project with the explicit aim of impacting the models of networking available to early career scholars. If I hadn't been ready to say yes and jump into this research project, I would have missed out on this collaborative and purposeful opportunity.

* *Panel discussions and symposiums:* I've had the opportunity to participate in national panel discussions and symposiums because colleagues have recognized that my work aligns with a larger community of research. Working with my doctoral advisor (co-author of this chapter) we have been accepted to present at multiple conferences this past year, affording me the opportunity to build a host of valuable skill sets aligned with the work faculty do at IHEs including presenting, serving as a session discussant, and networking with scholars in my field.

Purposefully crafting an academic identity and placing myself in a position where I'm pursuing my professional passions, combined with being an active and present member of my academic community, has afforded me the dual benefits of focus and opportunity. Of course, a little bit of luck (being in the right place at the right time) and a sincere willingness to embrace prospects as they have arisen have enabled me to capitalize on these opportunities. With all of the requirements, rigor, and expectations inherent within doctoral programs, trust me, it is tempting to say "no" when such opportunities arise. It can be overwhelming to take on greater responsibilities than your core program may require, but I have learned that it's well worth the additional effort to strategically consider any prospects for enhancing your academic work. When something presents itself that will both make a contribution to your field and concurrently serve your professional development within the framework of research, teaching, and service as you pursue your career as a member of a faculty in higher education – say "yes."

MAKING IT HAPPEN

Navigating the cultural and academic contexts of higher education across the US demands strategic and rigorous preparation. An understanding of institutional missions and how they shape faculty work is central to making timely and informed decisions regarding one's priorities. In our discussion of research, teaching, and service as the core of faculty life across IHEs, we have strived to communicate the critical importance of the nexus of passion and opportunity.

As the title of this chapter implies, the expectations for faculty work is ever increasing. Indeed, the bar is consistently rising in terms of the roles and responsibilities of faculty, and as noted, the notion of demonstrating impact has never been more pressing. Looking ahead, as you consider how to ensure your work will be impactful, we'd like to address an emerging trend in higher education – not necessarily a new trend – but one that has been developing steadily over a number of decades and one we feel represents a pathway to success. Building upon our perspectives of linking global education and mathematics, engaging in scholarship that transcends disciplinary boundaries is an excellent way to extend traditional lines of scholarship, seek meaningful and enduring collaborations, and consider outcomes with a greater potential for a broad impact. As discussed in Moss, Osborn, and Kaufman (2003), knowledge transcends both individuals and cultures and shifting toward an interdisciplinary approach to learning and teaching can foster new and exciting perspectives on historically compartmentalized disciplines. Thus, as our last bit of advice, we encourage you to seek opportunities for interdisciplinary work across the academy as representing what we believe to be a viable and productive pathway for success for you – the next generation of scholar-teachers.

ADVICE FROM FACULTY

In our final section, we would like to build upon our recommendations for engaging in the demands of complex faculty work by offering several brief narratives developed by our colleagues whose thoughtful approach to their work has inspired our own thinking and effort. Within the Neag School of Education at the University of Connecticut we are lucky to have mentors and colleagues that embody many of the very best attributes of scholarteachers and engaged citizens of the academy. To conclude our chapter, we'd like you to hear their voices directly as they offer enduring perspectives and advice that we believe will serve any aspiring early career scholar across their professional lifespan.

Todd Campbell – Professor, Science Education

> *One of my favourite quotes is, "People don't care how much you know, until they know how much you care." While I believe that success in higher education is multi-faceted and context dependent, in my experience across four universities over thirteen years in higher education, I have come to understand that a focus on caring can be most important. More specifically, the care and civility I have offered and received from colleagues and students and the care that I have approached my scholarship, teaching, and service with matter. While I have learned most of this personally through my own actions, a great deal of this learning has arisen from observing the success or demise of others that have surrounded me in higher education. Related to care and civility offered to colleagues and students, it has not been those colleagues that worked to position themselves as superior to others through their vast knowledge of*

*research literature and methodologies while treating
those around them as inferior that have had the
most success. Instead, thankfully, it has been those
colleagues that genuinely care about their co-
workers, their students, and the important role that
their scholarship, teaching, and service plays in the
larger mission of a just society that have found
success and in the end fulfilment. Given this, my
advice would be to let the care you approach people
and your work with be your most notable attribute.*

Mary Truxaw – Associate Professor, Mathematics Education

*If you are someone who came to academia later
than some (or later than many), recall that your
life experiences are valuable. Life experience can
ground you and help you to see what is worth
spending time pursuing and what might be less
important. Trust that you have plenty to offer …
then offer it. A gift of working in academia is that
you get to be professionally curious. Embrace
your curiosity. Look for theories and ideas and
questions that knock your socks off. If you are
wowed by ideas, they will sustain you and your
work. Collaborate with others – in the field, in the
classroom, in writing, in thinking. Shared ideas are
almost always better than ideas in isolation.*

Alan Marcus – Associate Professor, Social Studies Education

*Love what you do! It is critical as a doctoral
student and early career scholar to discover your
passions and to build your research and teaching
agenda around these passions. Being a professor
should not be a "job" but should be your own*

*personal mission built to achieve goals related
to your passions. In doing so, your dissertation,
courses, conference presentations, and publications
will not just be something to check off a list or used
for someone else's rankings but will be the way
you impact your field and carry on each day with
a smile. Love what you do in order to have a long,
happy, and satisfying career.*

ACKNOWLEDGMENTS

We would like to thank our colleagues and mentors in the Department of Curriculum and Instruction in the Neag School of Education at the University of Connecticut for their contributions and advice regarding the content of this chapter. We would also like to acknowledge the Office of the Dean for their support of U21 activities. This chapter is dedicated to our mentor and friend Megan Staples who approaches all of her professional work – and life – with a positive attitude of success.

REFERENCES

Gutstein, E., & Peterson, B. (Eds.). (2006). *Rethinking mathematics: Teaching social justice by the numbers*. Milwaukee, WI: Rethinking Schools.

Izard, B. (2018). Teaching Human Rights through Mathematics. *Mathematics Teacher*. *112*(2), 114–119.

Moss, D. M., Barry, C. A., & MacCleoud, H. (2018). Promoting intercultural learning through an international

teaching internship. In T. Huber & P. Roberson (Eds.),
*Second language learning and cultural competency in a
world of borders* (pp. 199–217). Charlotte, NC: Information
Age Publishing.

Moss, D. M., Osborn, T. A., & Kaufman, D. K. (2003).
Going beyond the boundaries. In D. K. Kaufman, D. M.
Moss, & T. A. Osborn (Eds.), *Beyond the boundaries: A
transdisciplinary approach to learning and teaching*
(pp. 1–12). Westport, CT: Praeger Publishers.

PART II

INTERNATIONAL PERSPECTIVES ON THE STRUCTURAL AND INSTITUTIONAL PROCESSES OF ACADEMIC PROMOTION

5

ACADEMIC PROMOTION IN THE UK: YOUR GUIDE TO SUCCESS

Jackie Cawkwell

INTRODUCTION

Academic promotion brings rewards to individuals but is also a critical measure of institutional quality: it is a positive indicator if colleagues successfully engage with rigorous scrutiny of professional practice and are rewarded through promotion. The drive and motivation toward recognition (extrinsically linked to public acclaim) and reward (intrinsically connected to personal terms and conditions of employment) is strong in academics, as in many other professional contexts, but has an unusual element in that the focus is on individual acclaim, rather than the more neutral business of job re-evaluation. Institutional commitment to academic promotion and enactment of policy has been ad hoc over the years in the UK and in the broader domain, higher education (HE) sector policy leaders have often demonstrated contradictions between demands for quality and reticence in terms of reciprocal reward. However, the relationship between individual contributions and institutional reputations is changing, with external quality frameworks of HE professional practice having a growing influence upon local promotion practice.

The focus of this chapter is on preparing for promotion once employed by an institution, rather than the challenging process of initially getting a step on the career ladder. It considers the professional academic practice of both teaching and research staff, with a particular focus on the complex pursuit of demonstrating effective teaching in HE. This is in response to the reality that metrics for evidencing contributions in research are much more established than for teaching. Attention is increasingly being paid, however, to the quality of teaching practice and a number of important influences are emerging that will inform local promotion policy which an individual must understand and, ultimately, exploit in terms of personal success. The professional role of an academic is also diversifying; familiarity and confidence with both teaching and research is a given for anyone wanting to pursue a long and successful career in academia.

The broad context of professional practice in HE is explored initially at UK sector level, followed by examples of local, institutional practice in academic promotion processes. The challenges of promotion and tips for success, identified by colleagues who have been recently successful, are then discussed. This is followed by a consideration of how an evidence-base might be established for demonstrating effective teaching practice; and the chapter concludes with a brief consideration of how the recognition of professional practice might be influenced by leaders of the future, with a reminder of some important pieces of advice to early career academics. While drawn from the UK context, key messages are relevant to broader, international, HE settings.

Although only a proxy for the measure of quality in universities, sector metrics concentrate the corporate university mind, often influencing targets for successful engagement, as well as the reward and recognition of professional practice. An effective understanding of this will be helpful in thinking about the impact upon your longer-term career plans.

THE UK SECTOR

Teaching Excellence Framework

The Teaching Excellence and Student Outcomes Framework (TEF) has been developed by the Department of Education for England and is notionally based upon concepts of metrics for measuring standards within the well-established Research Excellence Framework (REF). Optional for Wales, Northern Ireland, and Scotland, the framework is overseen by the Office for Students (a new agency which replaced the Higher Education Funding Council for England in March 2018) and is based upon three aspects of quality: teaching, learning environment, and student outcomes and learning gains. Still in its infancy, the TEF is rapidly developing into a significant driver for institutional teaching and learning priorities, drilling down to subject-level metrics after the initial implementation at institutional level. It will become increasingly important to pay attention to these metrics for assessing teaching excellence and student outcomes, as institutions align their own metrics for internal recognition to sector-wide measures for both teaching and research.

Full details of both the measures and process for the TEF assessment can be found in the UK Department of Education

(2017) website but for the purposes of evidencing more personal and individual contributions, a little more detail is given here:

- Teaching quality
  - o Student engagement
  - o Valuing teaching
  - o Rigor and stretch
  - o Feedback
- Learning environment
  - o Resources
  - o Scholarship, research, and professional practice
  - o Personalized learning
- Student outcomes and learning gains
  - o Employment and further study
  - o Employability and transferable skills
  - o Positive outcomes for all

Developing the capacity to reflect upon professional teaching practice in these broad terms and extending an evidence base to demonstrate impact in these areas will enhance and strengthen your future claims for recognition and reward.

Research Excellence Framework

The more established research equivalent for measuring quality is the REF (2018), overseen by the newly created UK Research and Innovation, and has been experienced for many years now within UK universities and has subsequently informed the deliberations and decisions of promotion committees. The REF assesses submissions based on:

- Quality of outputs

- Impact beyond academia

- The wider environment supporting research

It is worth noting that despite a growing acknowledgment of the value of teaching in universities, colleagues nevertheless have to demonstrate successful research practice within a claim for promotion: teaching is not worthy on its own to merit promotion. Thus, familiarity with the REF as a way of evidencing impact in your research activities, while also understanding its broader influence upon institutional values and metrics, is critical in anticipating the demands of local academic promotion policy and practice.

UK Professional Standards Framework

Another, established, UK HE sector framework for articulating teaching practice is also useful for shaping both continuing professional development planning and future claims for promotion. The UK Professional Standards Framework (UKPSF) is supported by a significant range of UK HE bodies and agencies and is growing in influence in international HE contexts. The framework has proved to be a robust and inclusive approach to recognizing the impact of professional practice in teaching and is effectively supporting individual recognition with the Higher Education Academy (HEA) Fellowships. In early 2018, the HEA (subsequently merged in March 2018 with the Equality Challenge Unit and the Leadership Foundation for HE into a new agency known as

Advance HE), recognized its 100,000th Fellow, confirming its value and extensive reputation.

More details on the UKPSF can be found at the HEA (2011) website but, in brief, the framework describes teaching and learning support within three key dimensions of practice:

- Areas of activity
    - o Designing learning activities
    - o Teaching and/or supporting learning
    - o Assessing and giving feedback
    - o Developing effective learning environments
    - o Engaging in continuing professional development
- Core knowledge
    - o Subject material
    - o Appropriate methods for teaching and learning in subject
    - o How students learn
    - o Appropriate learning technologies
    - o Evaluating effectiveness of teaching
    - o Implications of quality assurance and enhancement
- Professional values
    - o Respecting individual learners
    - o Promoting participation in HE
    - o Evidence-informed approach to practice
    - o Acknowledging wider context of HE

Again, developing an understanding of professional practice in such terms will help describe and corroborate claims for promotion. Gaining recognition as an HEA Fellow could also be a very valuable addition to your professional profile.

Researcher Development Framework

There is also a framework equivalent to the UKPSF in support of researcher personal, professional, and career development: the Researcher Development Framework (RDF) developed by VITAE (2010) which details the knowledge, behaviors and attributes of successful researchers in HE. This approach describes activities in terms of:

- Engagement, influence and impact

- Knowledge and intellectual abilities

- Personal effectiveness

- Research governance and organization

All these frameworks – TEF, REF, UKPSF, and RDF – offer ways of developing a common understanding of what effective practice constitutes and provides those responsible for career development and academic promotion with a way of planning for the realization of the future potential of the professional HE workforce. It could also be a useful exercise for you to reflect on the details within these four frameworks in order to identify features that are in common with your own teaching and research philosophy and practice.

Diversity of Academic Roles

Another aspect that is prominent within the UK sector and the academic role is diversification. In UK institutions, academic pathways commonly have a focus on one of the following three:

- Research

- Teaching and research

- Teaching

These pathways should be viewed as being more on a spectrum, rather than across a teaching/research divide as previously and you should familiarize yourself with the way the pathways operate in your own university. Successful HE professionals have to pay careful attention throughout an individual career to prevailing demand within an institution, across the HE sector in the UK and internationally. Accepted wisdom is to be flexible, responsive, and creative, not only in what you do, but also how you describe interventions and impact to others. This is equally true for you in your aspirations for promotion. In some cases, there will be also be institutional flexibility in moving between the pathways for promotion purposes; thus, a research and teaching post-holder, for example, may be successful in applying for a teaching-focused promotion, so long as their current practice can demonstrate sufficiently the required roles. This reinforces the message that flexibility and an open mind is always a good approach to adopt throughout your career.

THE UNIVERSITY

The marketization of HE in the UK, with the commensurate drive toward more transparency in transactions and outcomes, has led to a number of frameworks and metrics (cited above) which aim to establish the effectiveness of professional practice. In many ways this is constraining – these are not perfect measures for complex activities and can lead to reductionist targets and drivers – but they should also be viewed as an opportunity to define and discuss personal contributions within a shared language and as part of a broadly understood notion of excellence. It may take some time to shift the corporate mind toward these notions but the frameworks are there, the external drivers are there, and the demand for local recognition is there. Consequently, a critical task is to be familiar with the way that academic roles are defined and discussed in your local context; the language and distinctions in use can be one way of understanding the realities of local practice and professional culture. How is effective academic practice understood and valued in your institution? Understanding and describing individual professional practice in the same manner could be a good starting point for you.

Areas of Competencies within a Role

Universities will vary in specific detail, but, regardless of the academic pathway and regardless of the level of post, there will be professional competencies to address in an application. One example university (a Russell Group university) has three domains: teaching and learning activities; research and scholarship; and academic service and citizenship. This is very likely to be the case across a number of universities, although precise wording may differ slightly: be very clear on what your own institution requires. Continuing with the example university, most cases for successful promotion would demonstrate effective practice in all three domains although, exceptionally, sustained excellence in just one domain may be recognized for promotion. The key message here is that most commonly academics should be contributing effectively in all three domains. The balance across the three domains may vary but all should be evident to some appropriate degree. Consider how this might be achieved – are you a good all-rounder or do you excel in one domain more than the other two? Consider carefully what your focus is now and what your trajectory might be over time and keep sufficient diversity even if you consider yourself to be more of a specialist in one domain than the other. Being clear will help in terms of your professional development planning for the future and for the content of the application for promotion itself when you are ready. It is also increasingly common that some form of certification of HE teaching (such as a PgCert in Higher Education) or recognition of HE teaching (such as HEA Fellowship) be achieved before an application would be considered: check with your own university as it may be possible that requirements have changed since your initial appointment.

Role Profiles and Levels of Responsibility

Any university will differentiate between the pathway for an academic role (identified earlier as research, research and teaching, or teaching) and the level of responsibility (or role profile). In the example university again, these different role profiles are University Teacher, Assistant Professor, Associate Professor, and Professor; in another example (a modern, teaching-intensive university), these roles are Associate Academic, Lecturer, Senior Lecturer, and Principal Lecturer. Research Assistants, Post-Doctoral Researchers and Graduate Teaching Assistant roles can usually be found in both institutions. Familiarize yourself with the roles and the titles utilized by your university.

Also consider here the distinction between the ways of describing two core professional responsibilities within the different role profiles:

Assurance:

- University Teacher: work within the quality assurance framework and assume leadership roles as required, with support from senior colleagues.

- Assistant Professor: be responsible for and comply with quality assurance standards and procedures of academic area.

- Associate Professor: take responsibility for the quality assurance of programs of study.

- Professor: lead the development and clarification of academic standards for the subject area and quality assurance framework within the University's overall framework.

Enhancement:

- University Teacher: undertake formal development of practice and apply to practice.

- Assistant Professor: engage in scholarship and dissemination of teaching and learning.

- Associate Professor: engage proactively in the scholarship of teaching and learning by providing leadership of teaching and curriculum development, disseminating the results of this work both internally and externally in order to bring about positive change.

- Professor: engage proactively in the scholarship of teaching and learning, taking an evidence-based approach to curriculum development and implementation of new pedagogies, promote and market the work of the academic unit in the subject area both nationally and internationally.

You will be able to discern distinctions between responsibilities such as "taking an active role" (Assistant Professor); "developing practice" (Associate Professor); and "leading in strategic priority areas" (Professor). Being familiar with the increased levels of challenge for each responsibility for the different roles should help in distinguishing your own development needs and the language you should adopt in your application. Consider what the differences are, for example, between "broad" and "thorough" and "sustained" when it comes to ways of describing practice. Reflect the language used in such descriptors and benchmark yourself against these when writing an application or planning for a future application.

INSIGHTS AND GUIDANCE

A small-scale enquiry with successful applicants for promotion to Associate Professor and Professor conducted in a Russell Group university during 2016/17 identified a number of features that colleagues felt were pertinent to their achievement: challenges; support mechanisms; and tips for success. There follows a number of their ideas and insights.

Orientate yourself to the academic culture of both your disciplinary area and your local context. This may take some time but understanding the "language and values" will enhance the quality of your writing. There will inevitably be tacit knowledge and implicit understandings (as well as a possible gap between rhetoric and reality) of what is welcomed in terms of career development and your contributions. You may need to be prepared to challenge some of those assumptions and expectations, particularly if you are working in non-traditional academic areas, but do so in a respectful and positive manner if you are going to disrupt the norm. In a similar vein, you may also need to be prepared to explain why some impact measures of your contribution are different to those more traditionally expected for your discipline, particularly if you have a different academic background or are working in an inter-disciplinary context.

Also, consider carefully how your style of writing is perceived by members of a promotion committee. In some cases, humility and "reserve" do no favors when it comes to claiming success. Be clear and assertive about achievements and be very clear about what you individually contributed as part of a team effort and a shared outcome. On the other hand, think about perceptions of arrogance and boasting as cultural, gendered, and generational norms vary greatly. It could be particularly useful to ask a local colleague to read a draft from this perspective. Even with feedback before submission, it is possible that cultural sensitivities of senior colleagues prevent an honest appraisal because of the impact of your writing style. Also consider "voice" when it comes to your audience: qualitative feedback can be very powerful and can reinforce abstract quantitative data.

Develop a wide range of support mechanisms to help you persevere in what might possibly be challenging but, in any event, certainly a long-term endeavor. Nurture a group of critical friends and allies: obviously you want feedback that is sensitive but you also want it to be honest. Choose different colleagues and friends to comment on different aspects, playing to their strengths even if initially the feedback may be hard for you to hear. Further down the line, if you do apply and are not successful, decision making could also be more opaque than suggested by the local policy and guidance, so seek as much feedback as you can to support future applications. Also engage with any formal opportunities there may be to explain promotion processes, such as meetings that are convened by senior colleagues to reflect on work progress.

These may be called Professional Development and Progress Review meetings, or something similar, and are usually conducted annually with bi-annual updates. Put your ambitions for promotion onto the agenda even if your line manager is occupied with more short-term activities and outputs.

External colleagues are extremely important in validating your contribution; other experts in your subject area offer not only a great morale boost but could also support with future endorsements and inspiration. Nurture your external networks carefully and reciprocate with offers of support and ideas. And, critically, colleagues talked about developing a belief in yourself and the value of what you contribute. Benchmark yourself against external descriptions and requirements for new roles and also against other, more senior, colleagues within your own academic unit and beyond.

There were also many practical tips for success that colleagues identified to think about when applying for promotion, including:

- Word count: you obviously need to remain within any word count but also ensure that you do write up to the limit. If word count varies for the different sections, this implies that greater depth in some of your responses are expected and if you are well under the word count, the panel may think that you don't have enough to say about your contribution. Consider the delicate balance between concision and detail for a diverse audience of colleagues from disciplinary areas other than your own.

- Paperwork: make sure that you thoroughly understand the process, including what forms are required from both yourself and your advocates.

- Deadlines: give yourself plenty of time to draft, and re-draft again. When you ask colleagues to read your application and when you ask advocates to prepare their statements, you will also need to give them plenty of time as their feedback may suggest some changes to your claim.

- Evidence: expect this to take a long time to gather as some of the information may not be that easy to access even if ostensibly it is in the public domain of your team; for example, student feedback which may be held centrally and which may be difficult to collate.

- Reputation: you may operate in quite an exclusive academic field where recognition of your contributions may be beyond your local or institutional context. These reputations are nevertheless very valuable and influential, so think carefully about how you might effectively include in an application.

- Gaps: as you reflect upon the range of your contributions, you may spot areas that you have less, or no, experience in. Look to make good on this in time for your application.

- Be proactive: seek new out new opportunities to contribute and always say yes if asked to take on a new role; ensure the effort counts for you in terms of evidencing the impact of your contribution by keeping a journal or a log of activities; and always keep your professional CV up-to-date. So, be both flexible and strategic in your choices of new roles and responsibilities.

EVIDENCE BASE FOR IMPACT OF PRACTICE

Evidencing impact is difficult in any context and establishing that an intervention on your part has led to an enhanced learning experience and improved learning gains is notoriously complex. How can you credibly make a connection between the two? Simply stating an impact will not be sufficient: what objective measure can you draw upon to substantiate your claim? The evidence you seek may not currently exist in an accessible format, in which case you may need to gather new evidence yourself or prevail upon other colleagues to construct the information in the format you need. A range of metrics will also enhance your evidence base: think about different spheres of influence, including your own professional judgment, peer comments and feedback, senior colleague insights from within your institution and beyond, perspectives from associated professional bodies, external stakeholders and employers, as well as perceptions and feedback from your "audience" whether students or research recipients.

A more detailed discussion and scholarly exposition on the challenges of evidencing teaching achievements can be found in an HEA commissioned report "Promoting Teaching: making evidence count" (2013). This report specifically sought to offer guidance to HE institutions on promotion policy and practice to take teaching activities into account on a more equitable basis with research activities. Consequently, the report discusses how promotion committees might better understand the impact of teaching and how they might value this in local policies and practices. It is interesting to note that the report identifies different perspectives on teaching evidence from other frameworks discussed earlier (scope of activity, sphere of influence, and source of evidence) but the key message was to re-assure universities that the use of self-description and student surveys can in fact be verifiable and peer reviewed and as a result triangulated. The basis for demonstrating effective teaching practice continues to evolve in the UK but the HEA report was an important starting point for encouraging both individual practitioners (and sometimes their representative bodies) in calling for recognition, and institutions in more confidently measuring and rewarding contributions. For the purposes of this chapter, however, there follows a more practical look at what evidence might be developed and drawn upon to establish impact of HE teaching practice with both rigor and validity.

The approach to developing an evidence base to demonstrate effective practice is to think carefully about what feature of the learning experience you are claiming to have influenced and to draw upon as wide a range of objective verifiers as you can. Even if you are drawing upon your professional judgment and what feels like a subjective viewpoint, consider what has led to you taking that view and be clear that you are building upon activities such as professional experience, reflection, review, and the scholarship of teaching and learning as applied to your particular disciplinary context. Small-scale enquiries into teaching practice can be as influential as more complex pedagogical pieces of research, so be creative and innovative in your reflections and evaluations. Don't be afraid to refer to practices that may feel quite informal to you but which have contributed to the basis for making a judgment or taking a particular approach. In association with more quantitative data, you can begin to build a convincing basis for claiming effective practice.

Below is a range of ideas that you can develop as part of your reflective and evaluative practice and which will help you establish the veracity of your claim, in association with the endorsements that will also be required from internal and external colleagues. Table 1 has been adapted from an earlier piece of work by Crook (2016) and has been organized around the three domains of teaching and learning identified earlier, that is, teaching and learning, research and scholarship, and academic service and good citizenship. A fuller list

Table 1. Evidencing Teaching and Learning Achievements.

Theme	Definition	Examples of Practice
Teaching & learning: evaluation	Formal measures for good standing	Student feedback Peer feedback Alumni feedback External Examiner reports Recognition, such as HEA Fellowship or PgCert Higher Education Student teaching awards
Teaching & learning: innovation	Development of non-standard practice or resource	Assessment tools Teaching activities Forms of exposition Learning environments, such as WBL, independent and blended learning Technology-enhanced learning
Teaching & learning: development	Involvement in curriculum design and enrichment	New modules and programs New partnerships (internally and externally) New learning spaces

Teaching & learning: management	Institutional roles in support of teaching and learning	Module/Program Convener
		Member of School Committee
		Induction of new staff
		Staff mentor
		Placement tutor
		Exams officer
		Admissions tutor
		Student Services liaison
Teaching & learning: reflection	Encouragement of self-awareness and awareness of good practice	Peer observations
		External examining
		External course review
		Peer reviewer for pedagogic journals
Research & scholarship: subject research and scholarship	Contributions to knowledge and understanding of subject area	Undertaking research projects and enquiries
		Conducting empirical studies
		Presenting at conferences
		Publishing articles
		Contributing book chapters
		Editing journals
		Designing and organizing conferences or workshops
		REF outcomes

(*Continued*)

Table 1. (*Continued*)

Theme	Definition	Examples of Practice
Research & scholarship: pedagogic research and scholarship	Contributions to knowledge and understanding of teaching and learning in subject area	Undertaking research projects and enquiries Conducting empirical studies Presenting at conferences Publishing articles Contributing book chapters Editing journals Designing and organizing conferences or workshops
Academic service & citizenship: citizenship	Contributions outside of routine duties	Open days Widening participation activities Local community initiatives Student forums/SU events Covering for colleagues
Academic service & citizenship: collegiality	Collaborative relations with colleagues	Team teaching Joint PGR supervision Contributions to post graduate student Contributions to other teams outside of school
Academic service & citizenship: dissemination	Sharing of good practice	Sharing practice in social media Presentations to university committees Sharing with other teaching colleagues Presenting at teaching conferences Organizing teaching practice events Popular articles on teaching practice

Source: Adapted from Crook (2016).

of possible examples of activities associated with teaching and learning achievements can be found at the website detailed in the reference list at the end of this chapter.

Consider carefully how these examples are broad ranging and externally verified through peer endorsements and corroboration. It demonstrates that with a scholarly approach and attention to pedagogical practice, aspects of the student learning experience that may feel subjective can be developed into something more objective and robust. Qualitative, quantitative, and mixed-method research and inquiry conducted appropriately can be both insightful theoretically and offer pragmatic ways of improving practice. For an accessible and practical introduction to approaches to undertaking research in teaching and learning see Gray (2009). The table of evidence also demonstrates that the sphere of influence of an effective HE teacher is wide-ranging and not just within the sphere of the classroom; thus, contributions to the professions, to industry and to other external communities, for example, can all be valid measures of success. This often offers an effective lens through which to discuss previous professional roles in conjunction with current HE teaching contributions and roles.

LEADERSHIP

A final aspect to consider in terms of developing your professional practice for promotion is to consider what kind of an academic leader you want to be. There are many insights into, and perspectives on, effective leadership, although less commonly focused specifically on HE teaching and learning. One insight, offered by the Leadership Foundation suggests that "shared leadership may offer a means of reconnecting academics with a sense of collegiality, citizenship and community" and discusses the context, practice, and engagement of shared leadership (Bolden, Jones, Davis, & Gentle, 2015, p. 3). The core challenges, these authors argue, for the HE leader of the future is to foster a culture of innovation; model professional behaviors; support new and disruptive ideas; and allow space for "unfiltered" concepts. Gunn and Fisk (2013) also explore HE leadership through a literature review, concluding that there are a number of practices that effective leaders should employ: engaging the silent majority; influencing discussions on what colleagues feel is meaningful by introducing relevant material; and leading conversations in a scholarly direction. Briefly, these authors identify a number of themes on teaching leadership, including leading curriculum reform; implicit leadership; and distributed leadership. Which type of leader are you at present? What type of leader do you want to become? And what leadership contributions are valued by your institution?

ADVICE TO EARLY CAREER ACADEMICS

In support of your aspirations for future success, and reflecting on the key points within this chapter and conversations with colleagues who have been successful in gaining promotion, pay careful attention to how sector metrics and frameworks for both research and teaching are incorporated into your institution's policy and practice. Think how these more generic descriptions play out in your own practice and take advantage of any opportunities to gain a teaching qualification such as a Postgraduate Certificate in Higher Education or recognition from external organizations such as Fellowship of the HEA. Familiarize yourself with academic pathways, domains of practice, and role profiles within your university and develop an effective evidence base for demonstrating your contributions across the range of academic activities required. If you have any gaps in experience, seek to fill these through opportunities that arise or that you may create for yourself, and nurture both your internal and external professional networks to draw upon for support at a later stage.

CONCLUSION

The expansion of, and external scrutiny paid to, HE in the UK has led to a number of challenges as both institutions and individuals are increasingly required to establish a quality-assured contribution to the student learning experience. This has led to changing student behaviors and a growing demand for metrics with which to ostensibly measure success. Although not without criticism, this has also led to greater transparency in what is being measured and, thus, rewarded. This plays out at a more local and personal level with promotion policy and practice and offers opportunities to influence definitions of academic practice. Considerations of inclusivity and equality of opportunity are more willingly discussed and there is a growing shared language and understanding of what constitutes effective professional academic practice (such as the UKPSF for HE teachers and VITAE for HE researchers). There are also demands, quite rightly, for a re-balancing between the value and reward afforded to research and afforded to teaching, and a recognition that there are different, yet equally valid, ways of evidencing different academic activities. Perspectives on leadership in HE are also evolving and scrutiny increasingly being paid to behaviors and professional values, as well as knowledge and skills. Understanding the features and characteristics of these contexts and frameworks as they are played out in practice is critical in order to be in a good position for promotion in the future and for designing continuing professional development plans. Above all, think yourself into the professional domain you aspire to: never under-sell the work that you or your peers do, be flexible and creative in your use of opportunities to do new things, and behave as if that next leadership role is just around the corner.

REFERENCES

Bolden, R., Jones, S., Davis, H., & Gentle, P. (2015). *Developing and sustaining shared leadership in higher education*. Project Report, Leadership Foundation for Higher Education, London. Retrieved from http://eprints. uwe.ac.uk/27175/

Crook, C. (2016). *Teaching and learning achievements*. Retrieved from http://jcal.info/fss/FSS-S2-TL.html

Department of Education. (2017). Teaching excellence and student outcomes framework specification. Retrieved from https://assets.publishing.service.gov.uk/government/ uploads/system/uploads/attachment_data/file/658490/ Teaching_Excellence_and_Student_Outcomes_Framework_ Specification.pdf

Gray, D. (2009). *Doing research in the real world* (2nd ed.). London: Sage Publications.

Gunn, V., & Fisk, A. (2013). *Considering teaching excellence in higher education: 2007–2013: A literature review since the CHERI Report 2007*. Project Report, Higher Education Academy, York. Retrieved from http://eprints.gla. ac.uk/87987/1/87987.pdf

Higher Education Academy. (2011). UK professional standards framework. Retrieved from https://www. heacademy.ac.uk/system/files/downloads/uk_professional_ standards_framework.pdf

Higher Education Academy. (2013). *Promoting teaching: Making evidence count*. Retrieved from https://www. heacademy.ac.uk/system/files/making-evidence-count-web_0. pdf

Research Excellence Framework. (2018). *What is the REF?* Retrieved from http://www.ref.ac.uk/about/whatref/

VITAE. (2010). *Researchers professional development framework*. Retrieved from https://www.vitae.ac.uk/vitae-publications/rdf-related/researcher-development-framework-rdf-vitae.pdf/view

6

ACADEMIC CAREERS AND PROMOTIONS IN FINLAND AND AUSTRIA: SYSTEM AND INSTITUTIONAL PERSPECTIVES

Jussi Kivistö, Elias Pekkola and Attila Pausits

PROMOTIONS AND ACADEMIC CAREERS

Historically, academic careers in many European universities have been characterized by the civil servant status of academics (i.e., an open vacancy model) based on the German *Lehrstuhl* (professorial chair) tradition. The chair system has been abandoned in many countries, and the status of civil servants has been changed to private employment. At the same time, many European universities have introduced some variant of the tenure track model to increase the attractiveness of academic careers at their institutions; however, open vacancy models continue to dominate academic careers in Europe. This chapter describes the recent changes in the academic promotion systems of research universities by using case examples from tenure track models in two European countries: Finland and Austria. In conclusion, this chapter offers examples of best practices and challenges identified in the analyzed tenure track models and offers strategic advice for early career researchers.

ALTERNATIVE PROMOTION PATHS: OPEN VACANCY AND TENURE TRACK MODELS

In principle, academic career models – and, therefore, promotion systems – almost everywhere in the world can be divided into two major categories: "open vacancy" career models and "tenure track" career models (cf. Arnhold, Pekkola, Püttmann, & Sursock, 2017). The main differences between these models are related to the phases of entry and exit as well as the promotion methods. The open vacancy model is common in European systems that have been built in the state civil service tradition, whereas the tenure track model is the typical form of academic structure in Anglo American university tradition. In both models, many members of the academic labor force have atypical careers. Depending on their respective systems, educators may carry the following labels: non-tenured, contingent, fixed-term, project, or non-permanent academics (i.e., researchers, faculty members).

The open vacancy model is based on the concept that the number and availability of open positions or vacancies in universities determine the promotion possibilities. Entry into the open vacancy model can take place through various recruitment methods (e.g., selecting the best candidate who responds to a public vacancy, interviewing a restricted list of eligible candidates or making direct calls; Eurydice, 2017). Once a position is established or becomes vacant, it is open to all candidates at all stages of their careers, regardless

of the candidates' levels of seniority or institutional affili-
ations. Open positions can either be fixed-term or permanent employment relationships. In the case of permanent
positions, exit often takes place through the resignation
or retirement of the employee. Career "promotions" either
within the same university or at other universities are only
possible if a person leaves the position previously occupied
before assuming the new position. In some special cases, if
the employee leaves a position for a non-permanent position
that may become permanent based on a performance evaluation after a given time (e.g., three years), universities offer the
employee an option to return original position within a specific time frame. In such cases, universities hire someone for
the original position during the period that the new position
is not permanent (e.g., acting professor positions in Germany
[*Vertretungsprofessur*]).

Unlike the vacant position model, the tenure track model
provides a clear structure for academic careers; higher-level
positions can be secured after an evaluation without a resignation from the current position. The tenure track model is
often characterized by highly competitive selection processes
that occur at an early career stage – often the early post-
doctoral stage – and allows career advancement within or
from this position without the employee's resignation from a
previous position or recruitment to a new position. Although
there are several variations of the model, a tenure track model
is characterized by fixed-term contracts and "step-by-step,"
promotions during a probationary period, which usually
involves the hierarchical steps of assistant professorship, associate professorship and, finally, a full professorship (Pietilä,
2015). Advancement between the steps is usually based on
periodic reviews or evaluations of candidates' performance,
but these evaluations can also serve as exit points if a person
does not meet the threshold requirements.

Throughout Europe, the vacant position model is still the predominant system of recruitment and promotion for academia (Eurydice, 2017); however, the tenure track model, which is the standard recruitment and promotion model in American higher education, is gaining a stronger foothold in Europe. This trend is largely due to global competitive pressures. The main rationales for introducing a tenure track model are related to an aim of attracting a wider pool of talented junior candidates in global academic labor markets because it offers academics on tenure track a credible and straightforward vision of promotion prospects. At the same time, this model is risky; after the probationary period, if only the candidates considered qualified enough are promoted or granted academic tenure, those who fail are likely to face challenges in securing future academic positions. For many academics, job security in the form permanent employment is clearly one of the most important reasons to continue an academic career. Compared to the open vacancy model, therefore, the tenure track model can often be more rigid and demanding, have high productivity pressures and carry a realistic chance of stigmatizing failure (Pietilä, 2017).

ACADEMIC CAREER AND PROMOTION MODELS IN FINLAND AND AUSTRIA

Overall, a higher level of autonomy of universities with respect to academic careers and promotions seems to be a growing European trend. Still, in many European countries, at least some of the faculty members have the status of civil servants rather than private employees (Eurydice, 2017). There are broad differences between the historical career paths in Europe and other country-related specificities and elements among the types of higher education institutions – most notably, research universities and universities of applied sciences (Arnhold et al., 2017). Next, as an example of this diversity, the Finnish and Austrian career models and promotion practices are discussed in further detail.

Academic Careers and Promotions in Finland

Finnish academic careers and promotions have been (and still are) predominantly based on the open vacancy model. This can be explained by the fact that the Finnish university system has been developed according to the Humboldtian ideals and Lehrstuhl model (i.e., "chair" model) in which the role of the full, chair-holding professors was dominant until the 1990s. Promotion was previously only possible by application for vacant positions, which led to a career model that favored elderly, more experienced academics with accumulated merits (especially in senior lecturer positions) and made the competition unhealthy and promotions and career advancement unpredictable. Due to the fixed nature of the number and levels of positions as well as the traditional evaluation of research-based merits only, there was a certain level of stagnation and elitism. Other problems were career dead-ends for those who were not qualified to be professors at the time a professor's position became vacant, zero-sum competition due to the limited number of open vacancies, and little differentiation between professors related to their tasks and expertise.

In 2008, a working group commissioned by the Ministry of Education recommended the development of a "four-stage career model" for Finnish universities (Ministry of Culture and Education [MEC], 2008). The model was implemented at almost all universities after the Finnish legislative reforms of 2010; however, one exception was Aalto University, which relied on its own comprehensive tenure track model. At the same time, the contractual status of employment relationships was changed from civil servant to private employment at all universities. After that, the landscape of academic careers in Finnish universities changed considerably, particularly because:

- the majority of midcareer fixed-term positions (i.e., senior assistants) were converted to permanent positions of university lecturers or researchers;

- former assistant positions were changed to fixed-term positions of university instructors or doctoral students;

- the position of post-doctoral researcher was introduced and regularized; and

- as an alternative model for careers and promotions, the tenure track model was introduced in parallel to the open vacancies model.

Since 2010, Finnish universities have been free to establish or terminate academic positions independently. Despite this freedom, the open vacancy model has remained the dominant model for recruitments and, therefore, for promotions. This has meant still fewer promotion possibilities for young academics because the majority of the previously fixed-term midcareer positions (e.g., university lecturers, university researchers) were made permanent, and a limited number of new post-doctoral positions were established. At the same time, only a few mid-career positions were opened as tenure-track positions.

Currently, depending on the university, only 2–12% of open positions are based on the tenure track model (Välimaa et al., 2016). To a large extent, each university in Finland may determine the details of tenure track procedures (e.g., which actors to involve in recruitment and which promotion criteria apply; Pietilä, 2017). As mentioned, only one university, the private Aalto University, currently uses the tenure track model as its main recruitment and promotion model.

The tenure track model of Aalto University has attracted considerable international interest, and can be presented as a best-practice example of the Finnish tenure track system. The tenure track model at Aalto University[1] consists of three levels: assistant professor, associate professor, and full professor. See figure 1. Candidates for the tenure track can be recruited from any of these levels.

The tenure track model includes certain expectations regarding the amount of time and effort the candidates should devote to tasks related to the three missions (i.e., teaching, research, and service). As illustrated in Table 1, the expected emphasis on research or on artistic and professional work decreases, while the emphasis on service activities increases when a candidate moves toward full professorship.

Tenure track promotion proceeds according to three intermediate reviews: first term review, tenure decision, and promotion decision. For an assistant professor, it can take seven

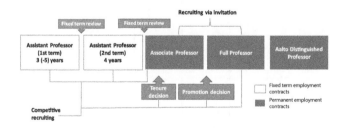

Fig. 1.   Tenure Track Model at Aalto University.
Source: Aalto University (2018).

Table 1. Expected Time Allocation at Different Stages of the Tenure Track.

	Assistant Professor (1)	Assistant Professor (2)	Associate Professor	Full Professor	Aalto Distinguished Professor
Research/artistic/ professional work	65% +/−10%	60% +/−10%	50% +/−10%	40% +/−15%	Negotiable
Teaching	30% +/−10%	30% +/−10%	30% +/−10%	30% +/−15%	30% +/−15%
Service	5% +5%	10% +/−5%	20% +/−10%	30% +/−15%	Negotiable

Source: Aalto University (2018).

to nine years before a tenure decision is made and a position of associate professor is secured. During the reviews, performance is evaluated based on three dimensions: (a) research and/or artistic and professional work, (b) teaching, and (c) service. The evaluation criteria are provided in Table 2.[2]

It should be noted that the Aalto University tenure track model is exceptionally well-developed compared to the tenure track models of other Finnish universities; however, it is likely that several Finnish universities will develop more comprehensive tenure track models in the future. Overall, due to the relatively short period of time allotted to apply for the tenure track at Finnish universities (i.e., only seven years), it is too early to determine whether there will be broader impacts of the tenure track model on academic career structures; however, thus far, some potential and actual strengths and weaknesses can be identified (Arnhold et al., 2017; Välimaa et al., 2016). The benefits of the tenure track system include the following: (a) improved management of risk associated with permanent positions through use of probationary periods; (b) the systemization of promotion practices; (c) a predictable motivational structure for tenure track faculty to reach the targeted goals; (d) the use of tenure tracks to introduce and strengthen new strategic fields of research; and (e) the ability to select a candidate with the best future potential without extensive requirements for accomplished merits. These benefits offer a solution to career dead-ends as well as internationally comparable and attractive options, thus allowing for a wider pool of recruits.

Tenure track systems, however, also have potential and actual challenges. For instance, if they are implemented only as an additional element of the open vacancy model, they strengthen the divisions between two ranks of academics. In addition, the tenure track leads to highly individualized motivational structures that may have negative impacts on collaboration, especially in teaching and organizational matters. The tenure track model also

Table 2. Evaluation Criteria.

Research and/or artistic and professional work	• The most important publications and their quality and impact, including the quality of the publication forums, from the viewpoint of the candidate's field of research; and/or the most important artistic works and their quality and impact. • Research/artistic work in other universities and research institutes or in professionally relevant positions (including doctoral studies and the postdoctoral phase). • The ability to build and lead a research/artistic team including possible doctoral students and postdoctoral research associates or artistic professionals supervised by the candidate. • The capability of raising competitive research funding or corresponding competitive funding in the artistic field. • The ability to conduct independent research/artistic work. *The following dimensions of research/artistic work are emphasized in the evaluation:* • International (and national) visibility and standing of the candidate and the team in the field. • Capability of raising competitive funding. • Achievements in doctoral education.

Teaching	• Teaching experience, including supervision of doctoral-, master-, and bachelor-level theses.
	• Development of teaching and experience in course development in the field.
	• Pedagogical education and studies.
	• The quality of student feedback.
	• Collegial feedback (e.g., head of department, director of degree program) and utilization of student and collegial feedback in developing teaching.
	• The ability to teach.
	The following dimensions of teaching are emphasized in the evaluation:
	• Achievements in doctoral education.
	• Experience in curriculum development.
Service	• The candidate's outreach and dissemination of her/his work.
	• Collaboration within Aalto University, schools, and the departments, such as committee, working group, and task force memberships.
	• Mentoring and coaching more junior colleagues.
	• Formal training on academic leadership.
	• Academic leadership positions, including committees and educational programs.
	• Service to the scientific/artistic community or society at large.

Source: Aalto University (2018).

requires strong human resource (HR) competencies and resources for developing the criteria for promotions and organizing assessments, and it requires more financial long-term planning; when introduced, it might initially lower the salary expenses of senior academic staff but will increase those salaries in the long-term.

Academic Careers and Promotions in Austria

Since the 1970s, the Austrian higher education promotion model could be described as an insider–outsider conflict in terms of academic career structures. Academics within the system ascended the career ladder and became civil servants because they were granted tenure of office (i.e., *Pragmatizierung*). It became difficult for younger academics to secure permanent positions at the universities. For those who worked at the universities for long periods, the institutions introduced the so-called "associate" or "extraordinary" professor positions without a tenure track model. This was a type of automatic promotion for distinguished scholars.

Over the past several years, academic promotions have become a key issue in higher education in Austria. Along with the new higher education legislation implemented in 2002, universities received more autonomy in terms of the planning, selection and development of their academic staff. Like Finnish universities, Austrian universities can freely make decisions regarding the promotion of (senior) academics as well as administrative staff. Establishing selection criteria at the faculty level, evaluations performed by a specifically formed selection committee and appointments made by decision-making bodies at the faculty and/or university levels are now common practices, which have reduced the external influence of the Ministry drastically; however, to open a position and hire senior academic staff (e.g., professors), universities must first negotiate with the Ministry regarding the three-year performance agreement. Newly established positions of professors, for example, must be agreed upon within three years for budgetary reasons.

Currently, there are two types of contractual status for the staff of Austrian universities: civil servants and private employees. The terms and conditions are different for the two groups. The number of civil servants is diminishing (i.e., currently at around one-third of total staff), and the number of private employees is increasing. Civil servant status will be phased out over the next 15 years as those with civil servant status retire. All new recruitment is based on private employee contracts (European University Association [EUA], 2017).

The institutional opportunities related to salary negotiations are also a key issue. First, the general collective agreement provides the framework for determining salaries and allows some freedom to "overpay" scholars with extraordinary reputations or to negotiate salaries with candidates; however, the collective agreement also regulates the negotiations between potential new employees and the university by using payment tables for the different staff categories. Second, due to the ongoing transition in the status from civil servants to private employees, Austria still applies the public service law for civil servants, including those who work at universities. In terms of academic promotion, this includes student co-workers, external lecturers (i.e., *Lektoren*), project staff, assistant and associate professors, university assistants and senior lecturers (internal) and university professors. These categories describe the different staff segments, clarify tasks, and specify academic qualifications. Promotions between these positions are both regulated by the national legislation and collective agreement and based on qualifications (e.g., PhD or habilitation as the qualification to conduct self-contained university teaching). Promotion regulations are also adopted within institutions as statutes.

With the revision of the legislation in 2015, Austria introduced a major change, which influences all areas discussed to some degree. University "docents" (i.e., scientific staff with habilitation) and Associate Professors can be promoted to University Professor positions with a "light appointment procedure." The procedures must include the qualification and job profile, the involved bodies, appointment criteria, decision-making approach, and other details; however, the legislation explicitly mentions that the procedures must be simplified compared to the traditional appointment procedures, which still exist. For example, this could mean that no external reviewers can take part in promotions, and that the promotions are determined by institutional administrative decisions. This specific approach closes the gap between the traditional tenure track and "Austrian tenure track" with no automatic promotion from associate to full or university professor. In contrast to the open vacancy model, this opportunity is reserved for only internal, highly qualified academic staff who lack the opportunity to pursue other career possibilities.

With a master's or diploma degree, a member of the scientific staff is first offered a university assistant position with a fixed term of four to six years. During this period, a doctoral degree should be achieved. This is where the Austrian system of tenure track model begins. As a post-doctoral employee,

Fig. 2.   Austrian Tenure Track Model.
Source: Adapted from Witzmann (2009).

the candidate can be promoted to a so-called "career position" for a maximum period of six years as an "Assistant Professor." This career position is based on a "qualification agreement" with the university. The agreement includes a number of expected outputs and achievements to demonstrate scientific quality and qualification (e.g., a specific number of publications, research projects or the habilitation of the candidate). If the agreement is fulfilled, the Assistant Professor is promoted to an associate position with a permanent position at the university. If a new university professor's position is opened, the associate professor can apply for that position but will not be automatically promoted to that position; therefore, the Austrian tenure track is not entirely comparable to the American tenure track.

Assistant Professors are granted freedom regarding their research and teaching and do not "belong" to a certain discipline-based chair. The evaluation that leads to an associate professor status is somewhat similar to the habilitation process in German-speaking countries. If the candidate fails the evaluation, the candidate's contract will be not renewed, and the candidate must leave the university. The advantage for those on a tenure track is that they will have already established a high level of independence early in their careers, enjoy collegiality and lenient decision-making structures, and depend less on university professors (e.g., teaching assistant activities). From an institutional perspective, the tenure track leads to a better student-professor ratio, and a higher level of academic output is ensured by the incentives established by the qualification contract; however, there is a need to balance the different types of professors within institutions. Currently, Austria has 2,190 University Professors, 759 Associated Professors, and 629 Assistant Professors. In addition, 2,120 are non-tenure track Associate Professors with habilitations (Bundesministerium für Bildung, Wissenschaft und Forschung [BMBWF], 2018).

In terms of academic self-governance and status, only Associate Professors belong to the group of Professors.

THE STRENGTHS AND WEAKNESSES OF CAREER MODELS IN THE CONTEXT OF PROMOTIONS

As has been discussed in the contexts of Finland and Austria, both the open vacancy model and the tenure track model have strengths and weaknesses as alternative models for academic careers and promotions. Table 3 summarizes the main insights presented in this chapter.

Both Finnish and Austrian universities face challenges in the future as they attempt to offer internationally competitive career models. In particular, promotions play a major role in the process of developing attractive academic career possibilities, therefore promotional opportunities should be considered factors that provide competitive advantages for institutions. European universities, which have clear, transparent, and well-documented promotion policies that are synced with the mission and profile of the institution, are likely to be more attractive employers than institutions in which promotion processes are not understood to be a crucial element in strategic staff development. Transitioning to the tenure track model requires stronger HR competencies, which can be a challenge for universities that are still in the learning phase regarding the process of becoming organizational entities separate from the state government.

ADVICE FOR EARLY CAREER SCHOLARS

It is important for the early career scholars to get into the regular career models (i.e., open vacancy or tenure track).

Table 3. Strengths and Weaknesses Associated with the Open Vacancy and Tenure Track Models.

	Main Strengths	Main Weaknesses
Open vacancy models	• Stronger role of academic profession in recruitments • Competitiveness in recruitment phase • Fairness (if open for all to apply) • Stability and autonomy of academic work • Low costs for staff development (external recruitments)	• Zero-sum competition • Career dead-ends • After selection, distraction from institutional mission • High risk of heavy recruitment processes to guarantee merit-based selections at all position levels • Focus only on merits, not potential • High risks of dissatisfaction of recruitment processes • Resignations and new recruitments in lower rank positions than professors • Little differentiation between professors related to their tasks

(*Continued*)

Table 3. (*Continued*)

	Main Strengths	Main Weaknesses
Tenure track models	• Stronger role of university management in recruitments and promotions • Stronger commitment to institutional mission, culture and processes • Shared values, independence, academic freedom • Promotion prospects within one university, no need to move to be promoted • Motivation through promotion possibilities • Focus also on best potential, not only past merits • No career dead-ends (if promoted) • International comparability and attractive option for international candidates • More independent from other professors in early career stages	• Strengthens the division into two ranks of academics • May highlight the research merits and other internationally comparable merits and neglect teaching and organizational merits • Creates highly individualized motivational structures • Potential for career dead-end (if not promoted) • Requires strong HR competencies and resources in developing the criteria for promotions and organizing the assessments

Getting into the track of atypical academic careers might be easier in the beginning, but transferring from it to the regular career track often can be very difficult. Unless having an atypical academic career is a desirable option, it is advisable that early career scholars be able to distinguish the "factual" career opportunities from "discursive" career opportunities. Sometimes, an early exit from an academic career can be a better option than getting stuck in the continuous, short, fixed-term contracts with few possibilities to gain merits necessary for regular academic careers.

Quite often, early career scholars have an idea of rational and linear career advancement based on research merits. This idea is rational, since academic career advancement, at least in the research universities, is research-driven. Nevertheless, it is important to also think about aiming for greater levels of diversity in skills and competencies. For instance, having a good command of generic skills such as management and coordination skills, social networking skills or interpersonal skills (e.g., cognitive flexibility and emotional intelligence) are assets and merits benefiting careers both inside and outside of academia.

Often, the importance of research merits is overly emphasized, and the importance of other merits is undervalued. Further, so-called service (third mission) activities including co-authorships (e.g., with colleagues from the business sector) or teaching in continuing education increases the scholar's own network outside academia. To develop the profile and portfolio of an early career scholar and to get additional competitive advantages in promotion (e.g., at another university), third mission activities might give the "little extra" needed for the scholar to land the new position. The academic world is changing quickly, however, and so are the requirements. For the majority, it is not enough to be successful in and merited in research; one also needs to be excellent and merited in other aspects surrounding the standard academic work.

Notes

1. The description of the Aalto University tenure track model is based on information derived from the university's public website: http://www.aalto .fi/en/about/careers/career_at_aalto/tenure_track/

2. A more detailed description of the policies and procedures of the Aalto University tenure track can be found at: http:// www.aalto.fi/en/midcom-serveattachmentguid-1e780d7 bbc3a6a280d711e799c3a15e0ace39123912/20160229_ tenuretrackpoliciesandprocedures_fi.pdf

REFERENCES

Aalto University. (2018). *Tenure track career system.* Retrieved from http://www.aalto.fi/en/about/careers/ career_at_aalto/tenure_track/

Arnhold, N., Pekkola, E., Püttmann, V., & Sursock, A. (2017). *Academic careers: Learning from good international practice.* World Bank. Retrieved from http://www.izm.gov. lv/images/izglitiba_augst/2_1_LV_Acad_Careers_Intern_ Practice_Report_FINAL.PDF

Bundesministerium für Bildung, Wissenschaft und Forschung (BMBWF). (2018). *Universitätsbericht. Wien: Bundesministerium für Bildung, Wissenschaft und Forschung.* Retrieved from https://www. bmbwf.gv.at/fileadmin/user_upload/Publikationen/ Universit%C3%A4tsbericht_2017_barrierefrei.pdf

European University Association (EUA). (2017). *University autonomy in Europe III: Country profiles.* Brussels:

European University Association. Retrieved from http: //www.eua.be/Libraries/publications-homepage-list/ university-autonomy-in-europe-iii-country-profiles

Eurydice. (2017). *Modernisation of higher education in Europe: Academic staff – 2017.* Eurydice Report, Publications Office of the European Union, Luxembourg. Retrieved from https://publications.europa.eu/en/publication-detail/-/ publication/40f84414-683f-11e7-b2f2-01aa75ed71a1/language-en

Ministry of Culture and Education (MEC). (2008). Neliportainen tutkijan ura. *Opetusministeriön työryhmämuistioita ja selvityksiä, 15.*

Pietilä, M. (2017). Incentivising academics: Experiences and expectations of the tenure track in Finland. *Studies in Higher Education.* doi:10.1080/03075079.2017.1405250 Retrieved from https://www.tandfonline.com/action/showCit Formats?doi=10.1080%2F03075079.2017.1405250

Välimaa, J., Stenvall, J., Siekkinen, T., Pekkola, E., Kivistö, J., Kuoppala, K., ..., Ursin, J. (2016). Neliportaisen tutkijanuramallin arviointihanke. *Loppuraportti. Opetus- ja kulttuuriministeriön julkaisuja* (Vol. 15). Helsinki: Opetus- ja kulttuuriministeriö. Retrieved from http://julkaisut.valtio neuvosto.fi/bitstream/handle/10024/74897/okm15.pdf

Witzmann, E. (2009). Junge Wissenschaftler werden ausgehungert. *Die Presse.* Retrieved from https:// diepresse.com/home/politik/innenpolitik/464809/ Junge-Wissenschaftler-werden-ausgehungert

7

THE ACADEMIC MARKET IN LATIN AMERICA: CHALLENGES AND OPPORTUNITIES FOR EARLY CAREER SCHOLARS

Elizabeth Balbachevsky

INTRODUCTION

Latin America is a vast and diverse continent. Not only are there dozens of different nations but each country is also marked by stark regional differences. Nevertheless, the academic profession in all countries shares some common features that are important for an emerging scholar to know. Here, maybe more than in other parts of the world, early career decisions have significant and long-lasting consequences. This chapter presents the Latin American academic context focusing on the academic career ladder, as it is organized both in the public and the private sectors, exploring the many sources of tension and challenges, as well as opportunities for early career scholars in the region.

HIGHER EDUCATION IN LATIN AMERICA

Latin America extends through three continents: North America, Central America, and South America, and comprises more than 20 countries. Each of these countries has its own higher education system, characterized by different balances between public and private institutions, the institutional arrangements for research and graduate education, and particular policies for quality assurance and academic personnel. In some countries, such as Argentina, Chile, Peru, and Mexico, higher education is a very old and engrained experience, with universities dating back to the early colonial period (mostly sixteenth century). In other countries, including Uruguay, Paraguay, and Brazil, higher education is considerably more recent.

By taking a broad approach, however, it is possible to point out some general trends and historical dynamics shared by all higher education systems in Latin America. To a certain degree, all were profoundly reorganized (or created) following each nation's independence, during the first half of the nineteenth century. At that time, establishing universities was part of the ambitious project of building modern nation-states out of the old colonial heritage. Universities were then charged with the responsibility of providing the new countries with the professional elites, trained according to the best technical and legal knowledge available (Schwartzman, 1993). Accordingly, in almost all countries, higher education was reformed to a heavily centralized and elitist approach, where universities are licensed by the state to teach and certify established professions, following strict curricula defined by the central Government.

From these institutional dynamics come some very important traits that one should have in mind when approaching higher education in Latin America. First, one should notice the centrality and traditional relevance of the bachelor's degree. In fact, academic life in most Latin American universities tends to gravitate around this all-important first-level university degree. It defines the core identity of most Latin American academic personnel. Also, in many countries, for most of the nineteenth and twentieth centuries, the bachelor's degree was the only kind of degree Latin American universities granted. Graduate education (master's and doctoral programs) are a late addition to this institutional fabric, and in most countries, still play a small role. In fact, only in Brazil and Argentina could graduate education be considered consolidated. Even so, only in few universities in Brazil graduate education is a major enterprise, being responsible for more than 25% of all enrollments. In the beginning of the twenty-first century, Chile, Peru, and Cuba also started more significant programs designed to enlarge and improve graduate education, both in terms of size and quality.

The heritage of heavily centralized institutions has made the traditional Latin American university a teaching-centered institution. While research has developed since the 1970s, its institutional locus represents an ad hoc addition to the formal institutional design. Research tends to be organized in isolated laboratories and centers. Thriving in these protected environments, research sustains weak links with the core activities carried out by most of the academics, which gravitate around teaching in the bachelor's programs.

This institutional heritage also helps us to understand the roots of some peculiar traits of the academic market in Latin America. First, in a teaching-centered system focused on providing professional training, it is easy to understand why part-time contracts are so widespread, even in traditional and well-regarded universities. In this context, the traditional professor was (and still is) the distinguished professional that also teaches in university. Accordingly, the academic activity is a secondary (while highly prestigious) occupation, the crown of a well-established and reputable professional career that allows the professional to influence the training of new generations of professionals. Second, it is possible to see why graduate degrees have a limited position within the structure of the academic career in most of the Latin American universities. Traditionally, it is the bachelor's degree that defines the academic's identity, and the career is carved inside the university, as the professional builds up their prestige in the country's intellectual and professional circles.

Finally, by its nature, the academic profession was thought to be an open system, and professional standards are controlled by the external mechanisms that organize the professional market. The academic market is mostly organized into closed internal markets (Musselin, 2005), where promotion occurs within the university, following a hybrid set of criteria which combines criteria produced by academic activity with those produced by professional performance. Also, traditionally, access to an academic position was subject to a lengthy screening process where a candidate started the academic life informally, collaborating with an established professor (in some cases, even on a pro-bono basis). This collaboration created opportunities for the candidate to build up a reputation little by little, as their involvement with the academic life deepened.

THE NEW DYNAMICS OF THE TWENTIETH AND TWENTY-FIRST CENTURIES

Since the second half of the twentieth century, the traditional institutional fabric of Latin American higher education has experienced a number of changes that altered its profile, firstly there has been large growth. Since the 1970s, access to higher education has been expanding in all Latin American countries. Even if some countries still lag behind, most of them have already reached the level of enrollments that characterizes a mass higher education system (Trow, 1973, 2000), and some have even reached levels of access that could be considered universal. Responding to these dynamics, Latin American higher education (HE) grew and differentiated; in some countries it was the public sector that answered the first demand for access, in the 1970s, which gave rise to exceptionally large universities, known as mega-universities, with hundreds of thousands of students enrolled in massive bachelor's programs. In other countries, this demand was adopted by the private sector.

Both trajectories produced strong differentiation and hierarchies in the Latin American HE landscapes: in the countries where the public university responded to massification, private education grew by initially catering for students from upper-middle class backgrounds, interested in the selective social environment offered by such institutions. In countries where the private sector led the way, the public universities were preserved from the most deleterious effects of massification and remained as an alternative for training the elites. As new waves of growth hit these systems, new dynamics fomented processes of consolidation in the private sector, opening space for a new institutional profile: the private demand-driven conglomerate, some of which are openly defined as for-profit organizations by the national laws.

The waves of quick expansion of higher education, in both public and private sectors, and the small size of graduate education, led to the hiring of a large number of new academic staff with shaky academic and professional credentials. Contrary to the old model of professor which was also a professional, these academics are entirely dependent on the academic market to earn their living, even when they only have access to part-time contracts. If this is the case, they opt for teaching in several institutions in order to assure a reasonable income. They often have little training, both in terms of research and teaching competences, and are unable to establish a personal academic reputation. Due to this they band together into radical unions to fight against the new policies adopted by some Latin American countries in recent years, which target academic credentials and research performance (Balbachevsky, 2016).

The second change came from the advent of research as a second mission of universities. The quest for research and research-related training in Latin America has a long tradition, dating from the Cordoba Student Movement, in 1918 (Bernasconi, 2007). Nevertheless, it was only at the beginning of the 1960s that the push for research-related activities gained true impetus, when the first generations of internationally trained PhD holders came back to their former institutions. Most of these early career academics left their country already holding place in public (and some prestigious Catholic) universities. They went abroad via scholarships, and came back poised and experienced to support research; including logistics, grants, and full-time contracts. In most countries, they settled into laboratories and research centers loosely appended to the university's main institutional fabric. Inside these protected environments, these academics were able to create dynamic centers of excellence devoted to the advancement of basic science, and supported by public money funded by the newly created National Councils for Research organized in most countries of Latin America at the end of the 1960s, under the influence of UNESCO (Davyt García, 2001).

In some countries, these research-oriented environments also evolved to nurture training programs and graduate education, especially doctoral programs. Here, the most successful case is Brazil, where a new layer of graduate training, supported by a well-developed peer-review based evaluation, emerged from these initiatives. Here graduate education, particularly PhD training programs, is supported by dedicated public funds and regulated by a Federal agency. With this support and regulation, Brazilian PhD training developed into one of the largest systems in the world.

These historical processes explain why it is quite usual to find enclaves of research-oriented micro-environments inside almost all Latin American universities, even the most teaching oriented ones. These enclaves function as a barrier, isolating and protecting the research group from the worst bureaucratic norms coming from the institution as a whole, and sometimes create very dynamic environments.

These processes also help us to understand why, in Latin America, universities don't commonly invest institutional money into research – although they may support graduate education. Traditionally, universities see themselves as teaching institutions, and in many cases, employ academics in part-time contracts considering only the time they devote for teaching (in some cases, only teaching in bachelor's programs), while research support comes from the National Councils for Research, in the form of research grants for supporting specific projects and scholarships. This reality created a very particular profile of academics intensively devoted to research, more or less oblivious from the bureaucratic regulations imposed by the university as a whole, and with a strong entrepreneurial profile, constantly in search for new sources to support their Center or Laboratory. In the words of a senior Mexican researcher interviewed in 2006:

> *I have to play the role of managing the search for*
> *the project's financing resources that allow us to*

> *maintain the laboratory and the people that work*
> *here: grants for the students to continue their*
> *studies, payments to students who stop having*
> *grants, payments of the laboratory technicians, and*
> *specialist maintenance personnel for particular*
> *situations, assistance for field work, conferences, etc.*
> *(quoted in Balbachevsky, 2008, pp. 31–32)*

Both changes – massification and the advent of research – created dynamics of differentiation and stratification in the academic market in almost all countries in Latin America. Institutional stratification was reinforced by the differential institutional commitment to research and teaching, and by the clientele attended by the institution: demand-driven or elite oriented institutions. Also, in many countries and institutions, these changes gave rise to an intense differentiation and stratification in the internal markets, inside the same university: full-time permanent places are found side by side with part-time, even per-hour paid positions. As I will argue below, while changing from one internal market to another is easier at the beginning of the career, it becomes increasingly difficult later in academic life. Also, while the Latin American academic market allows for a degree of mobility at the beginning of the career, later, the academic faces significant challenges in changing their institutional affiliation. This situation arises not only because each trajectory produces different outputs, but also because many of the benefits accrued later in academic life are dependent on seniority.

THE ACADEMIC PROFESSION IN CONTEMPORARY LATIN AMERICA: A LAYERED PROFESSION[1]

The dynamics described above ended up creating a highly diversified and stratified academic profession, where different profiles are superimposed, even inside the same institution. Each profile has roots in different phases of the history of HE and is perpetuated by different mechanisms supporting expansion, diversification, and stratification. In order to understand the more relevant differences opposing these profiles, I propose a typology considering two different aspects that organize the day-to-day academic life in Latin America: the degree of congruence between the academic rank occupied by an academic and their academic credentials, and the academic's degree of engagement with research.

The two dimensions proposed above allow us to identify four different academic profiles present in Latin America universities: first, there is the *old academic oligarchy* composed of academics with weak academic credentials, but placed in positions of authority inside the university. Some of these correspond to the traditional professor as described above: a distinguished professional who also teaches in a university and holds a high rank inside a professional school. Others are academics with no particular professional identity, but with large experience in the bureaucratic rules by which the university is organized, and who used these rules in their favor to assure access to a higher position inside the academy.

Second, there is the *academic elite*, composed of scholars with good academic credentials and well positioned in the institution's academic ladder. These academics are usually research leaders and center directors. Their daily life revolves around the research center or laboratory where they concentrate their academic activity. For them, autonomy is a key issue; only strong, autonomous research units are capable of resisting the interferences coming from the more or less politicized environment that is traditional in the Latin American university (Schwartzman, 1993). In many universities, while academics with this profile are capable of protecting their small research environment, they do not control the rules of the university as a whole, making it difficult for them to assure that their collaborators have access to stable academic positions.

Third, there are the *early career scholars*: academics with good academic credentials – usually a PhD – and strong commitments to research and knowledge creation, but positioned in the lower ranks of the universities. For different reasons, in their cases, research and commitment to academic life have not been translated into institutional recognition. They share the core values expressed by the academic elite, but are more vulnerable to pressures coming from the unions and radical views sustained by political movements from society. If they find employment in a more research-oriented university, or happen to be affiliated to a strong research center or laboratory, their career prospects are good. However, the lack of a research-oriented environment in their area can easily result in a frustrating academic life, where research becomes an individual endeavor, limited by the lack of funds and the lack of institutional support, resulting in products of low impact and recognition.

Finally, for the majority of *lecturers* in Latin America, the lack of academic credentials and little or almost no experience with research produces a profile more similar with the teacher at the secondary school than the one the international literature usually identifies as the academic scholar. Even if teaching at universities, they stay almost entirely disconnected from their national and international peer communities. Hence, their professional identity is neither defined by their professional degree, as is the case of the traditional professors, nor by their achievements as scholars. Instead, their identity is locally rooted, based on their institutional affiliation and the small group of colleagues with whom they share their daily life. In a sense, academics belonging to this group tend to sustain a "semi-professional identity" (Etzioni, 1969) since they tend to emphasize intrinsic rewards like personal satisfaction as opposed to extrinsic ones, like peer recognition or professional status. This explains why this group so fiercely opposes any attempt to introduce intra- and inter-institutional differentiation based on merit and/or prestige in Latin America. For them, the only acceptable grounds for differentiation are those produced by externalities, in principle accessible to everyone, like seniority.

ENTERING THE ACADEMIC PROFESSION IN LATIN AMERICA

Because of this highly differentiated and stratified profile of the academic profession in Latin America, early career decisions may have lasting effects for the early career academic. A single decision could entangle the early career scholar in a dead-end situation from which it is hard to be extricated later. Not only it is necessary to consider the institution's profile and reputation, but also the field's configuration inside a particular university.

For an early career scholar holding a doctorate, to be attached to a strong research environment (a laboratory or a research center), supported by a researcher leader with a good reputation and experience in garnering research and funding support is the best option. A provisional position as a research assistant or even a post-doc scholarship is a good starting point for this route to the academic market, even if it is never an assured one.

However, one thing is to find an informal position inside such environments, working alongside a good research leader.

Another thing is to be hired as part of the university's academic staff. Many early career scholars start a promising career working with a scholarship or a grant inside a research team but end up more or less confined into a situation of permanent informality, without stable or permanent employment within the university. This situation happens because in most universities research centers do not have control over academic places, which are supposed to belong to departments and programs. And one should never underestimate the shadow resistance posed by the old oligarchy and the early career lecturers to changes that would make the university environment more dynamic and competitive. A change of this nature is seen as a threat to their power and weakens their assured position. So, another thing to consider is the balance of power between the old oligarchy and the new academic elite. The larger the control of the oligarchy over the higher ranks inside the university, the bigger the challenges faced by early career scholars in their attempts to find a more stable position. An early career lecturer, without proper academic training represents a much preferred alternative in their eyes.

Another route for an early career scholar to gain a stable position is to search for opportunities in a teaching-centered institution. Regional public universities or some upcoming private institutions open new positions at the beginning of the academic ladder from time to time. And in most countries, access to these positions is achieved through a formal contest. Even if the academic oligarchy is not committed to selecting the best, formal norms and policies enforced by the government may create opportunities for better qualified academics. An early career scholar could start their career here, and, with luck, find support for their research activity, creating opportunities for accumulating credentials and academic outputs that would later strengthen their bid for a subsequent position in a more research-oriented institution. Nevertheless, in the academic environment of a teaching-centered institutions, the early career scholar may face a challenging environment, with poor career prospects and even some open resistance to their engagement in research coming from the less qualified colleagues. Also, in Latin America, access to research grants has become increasingly competitive, which can create obstacles for bids from isolated recent doctoral graduates. The best (but less accessible) alternative in these situations is to attach one's project to a collective research effort organized inside a major national research network. However, opportunities for this kind of networking are rare and are critically dependent on the connections the early career scholar forged in their doctoral years. Thus, the success of this route is strongly dependent on the connections the academic had built in their years of training.

A very different tale describes the challenges faced by an early career scholar that attended a post-graduate program *after* being accepted as part of the academic staff in a university. This is quite a common trajectory in many countries in Latin America, where opportunities for attending a graduate program are not widespread. For these academics, the main challenge comes before starting the program in being able to disentangle themselves from the teaching and administrative duties that usually burden their daily life for attending a graduate program. Once their bid for a leave to study is accepted, it is easier to find some support for the study period. In fact, many Latin American governments have scholarship programs targeting this profile of candidate. Once coming back, the emerging scholar will face similar challenges as described above; the less research-oriented their institution, the more difficult it will be to become established as a scholar engaged in research and graduate education.

Finally, the last option is to accept a per-hour paid position as teacher in the private sector or to be a part-time teaching assistant to a mega-university (public). This is the least desirable option for many. Holding this kind of appointment means the new/emerging scholar would not qualify for a post-doc scholarship, which always demands full-time commitment. On the other hand, the low-paid position means that it will be necessary to accept large teaching loads (sometimes as large as 30 hours per week) and even find another part-time position in a different institution. With this route, it would be impossible for the early career academic to amass the experience and academic outputs necessary to make them competitive in any opportunities for a more stable or permanent position, either in the public sector or in the elite-oriented private institutions.

CONCLUSION

This chapter explores how past heritage and recent changes in societal and policy environment shape the academic market in Latin America. As in many emerging countries, these contradictory dynamics create strong dilemmas for an early career scholar. Not long ago, academics in Latin America were hired as assistants, holding only a bachelor's degree. Then it was possible to design a post-graduate training path after securing a stable position inside a public university. This was my experience, as an example. While this route is still possible in universities situated in more remote regions, the challenges for building a productive academic career afterwards is much more difficult. If the academic wants to go on living in more central regions, the beginning of the academic career is full of hidden traps. Here, while attending a graduate program has become essential, it is not an assurance for a good placement, leading to a satisfying academic life, being it in the private or public institutions. While in the central regions one can find different job alternatives, one should always have in mind that earlier career decisions cast a long shade in the prospects for the future. The window of opportunity that could lead to a placement with good prospects for healthy academic development is small. Once locked into a path leading to a poorly endowed academic life, changing trajectory is extremely hard. The dynamics of segregation that separate vibrant from staled academic environments impose strong barriers for changing routes later in academic life.

Note

1. This section is mostly based on Section 6.3 of Balbachevsky (2016, pp. 106–108).

REFERENCES

Balbachevsky, E. (2008). Incentives and obstacles to academic entrepreneurship. In *University and development in Latin America: Successful experiences of research centers* (pp. 23–42). Rotterdam, The Netherlands: Sense Publishers.

Balbachevsky, E. (2016). The academic profession in Latin America: Between a corporatist and a professional ethos. In *Trends and challenges in science and higher education* (pp. 103–117). Dordrecht, The Netherlands: Springer.

Bernasconi, A. (2007). Is there a Latin American model of the university? *Comparative Education Review*, *52*(1), 27–52.

Davyt Garcia, A. (2001). *Avaliação por pares e processo decisorio nas agencias de fomento a pesquisa. O CNPq e a FAPESP*. UNICAMP, State University of Campinas,

Campinas, SP, Brazil. Retrieved from http://repositorio.unicamp.br/jspui/handle/REPOSIP/286881

Etzioni, A. (1969). *The semi-professions and their organization: Teachers, nurses, social workers* (1st ed.). New York, NY: Free Press.

Musselin, C. (2005). European academic labor markets in transition. *Higher Education*, *49*(1–2), 135–154.

Schwartzman, S. (1993). Policies for higher education in Latin America: The context. *Higher Education*, *25*(1), 9–20.

Trow, M. (1973). *Problems in the transition from elite to mass higher education*. Princeton, NJ: Carnegie Commission on Higher Education. Retrieved from https://files.eric.ed.gov/fulltext/ED091983.pdf. Accessed on February 20, 2018.

Trow, M. (2000). From mass higher education to universal access: The American advantage. *Minerva*, *37*(4), 303–328.

8

PROMOTION WITHIN
THE ACADEMY

Graeme Aitken

Promotion[1] is, and should be, a serious business. At its center lie the values of the institution and the hearts and minds of its staff. Done well it is affirming and aspirational. Done poorly it can be confusing and demoralizing. So what does it mean to "do it well"?

TYPICAL PARAMETERS OF PROMOTION

The promotion process is an assessment by peers. Like all assessments it should start with clear communication of expectations. Commonly these expectations center around teaching, research, and service (sometimes named as leadership or professional engagement). But the specification of these expectations is not always straightforward.

There are many widely used and well-regarded metrics and conventions for assessing research quantity, quality, and impact (e.g., publisher reputation, journal rank, acceptance rates, citations, h-index, i10-index, RG score, and, less commonly perhaps, uptake of practice by a professional community or incorporation of research into policy). Research funding is also a relatively straightforward matter to consider both in terms of value and source (with highly contestable and prestigious given the most weighting). Depending on whether it is regarded as teaching or research doctoral supervision completions are another easily quantifiable metric of research strength.

The metrics for teaching and service are less well-defined, however, and this can create confusion for those seeking promotion.

Given that the ultimate goal of teaching is to promote learning it makes sense to consider evidence that relates to the student experience of learning. This is often short-cut in promotion processes to student evaluation scores giving them a dominance that is not fully representative of the teaching endeavor. Students are good judges of whether teaching is challenging, interesting, and clear but they are less well-equipped to decide whether what they are taught is accurate, whether it addresses the most important ideas in the discipline and whether the introduction of these ideas is appropriately sequenced. The other most commonly used measure of teaching is peer observation. Peer reviewers, especially those familiar with the discipline, can balance the deficiencies of student feedback by commenting on areas that students cannot – accuracy, prioritization and sequencing of content – but they have only very limited access to the extent to which students are engaged and learning. Typically peer observations are one-off and as such they represent a very limited sample of teaching. Furthermore, what is observed is potentially atypical because it is natural to prepare even more thoroughly than normal for an observation that is foreshadowed.

Promotion that places a heavy reliance on student evaluations and on one-off peer observation misses much that is of value in teaching – program, course, and assessment design; experimentation with new approaches to improve learning; reflection on and action in response to feedback from students and from multiple, collaborative peer observations focused on a particular teaching challenge; reflection and action on student performance on assessment tasks, and on changes between pre and post assessment; and the sharing and dissemination of teaching challenges and ideas with peers. A well-considered application for promotion should address all of these elements. Teaching also has an important administrative component – being well-organized and on time, being clear about expectations so students time is not wasted on confusion and uncertainty, and prompt marking of work.

Service is even more intangible than teaching when it comes to measuring its contribution to promotion. Service has an outward focus toward our discipline, the practice communities with whom we work, and the policy environment, and an inward focus toward our own institution. Service, especially internal service, is often misunderstood as simply attending meetings. Service that supports promotion needs to emphasize contribution and influence – not just that you served on a committee but what you contributed and what difference it made. Given the multiple pressures on academics in the early stages of their career the weighting given to service is often less than the weighting allocated to research and teaching with the focus largely on local service (at the Department level) and collegiality.

ENTRY INTO THE ACADEMY

The chapters of this book describe the promotion perceptions and experiences of early career academics. They offer salutary reminders that the parameters of promotion described above do not always play out in a tidy and equitable way. Whether consciously conceived or not the parameters are largely premised on the assumption of an uninterrupted academic pattern of undergraduate degree, master's, PhD and into the academy, and on undifferentiated access once in the academy to teaching, research, and service opportunities. But as the prior chapters of this book illustrate this is far from the case.

Entry into the academy is a complex and often uncertain process. For many, entry begins with an insecure foothold. Some secure a start through research assistant work during their PhD program, often through the good fortune of being attached to a supervisor with research funds. Others, through work as graduate teaching assistants. But in neither case is employment secure. The research funding is often only short term and teaching opportunities are also dependent on student enrolments and discretionary funding. And nor is it complete in the sense of the expectations of the academy. It is rare that entry through graduate teaching offers research opportunities or that entry as a research assistant offers teaching opportunities.

There are other pathways but these too have their insecurities and uncertainties. Post-doc or research fellow opportunities typically offer the prospect of a two or three-year contract so have more security than temporary research assistant and graduate teaching work. But at the end there is no promise or permanence and employment prospects can be limited by a lack of experience of teaching. Some find their way into the academy from other employment – from working in administrative positions in the university but with a growing interest in contributing as an academic, or from a professional background. While those entering this way may have more security if appointed to a tenured position there are often considerable complexities to be negotiated. Foremost among these is that most who enter through this pathway find themselves for reasons of personal interest and academic credibility completing postgraduate or doctoral study alongside a full teaching and administration load. The urgency and importance of the demands of teaching compete with the importance but less urgency of the demands of research and compromise the timeframes for doctoral completion which generally makes this a slow way into academy. It may also, depending on the sort of employment contract, offer a restricted entry into a teaching-only pathway with no longer term prospects for research and therefore for full promotion.

Compounding each of these ways into the academy and the associated prospects for promotion is the often interrupted nature of the experience as a result of family responsibilities and the need, if not employed within the academy, to earn money to live on.

NAVIGATING THE PATH TO PROMOTION

Given the realities of entry to the academy how can early career academic best negotiate the path to promotion? Many of the chapters in this book offer practical and useful advice from the authors themselves and from their experienced colleagues. Much of this I will reinforce here. Based on nine years of experience chairing a promotion committee in a research-intensive university I offer the following observations but with the caveat that these are based on experience in one university and in one country's university system. One of the strongest messages in this book is that what it means to be in the academy, and to enter it and be promoted within it varies considerably.

Document as you go – irrespective of the rocky pathway into the academy make sure you document as you go, and in a systematic way, what you have contributed. This includes documenting the contributions you made, or are making, in your short-term contract positions as a research assistant or a graduate teaching assistant. One of the burdens of making a promotion application is having to recall everything you have done often over a very long period of time. This burden is often evident in applications that simply comprise long lists of activities, or that are long and discursive. Bear in mind that promotion committees are usually reading large numbers of applications. Systematic recording against the criteria for promotion in your university make it more straightforward for you to ultimately write a clear, concise, and focused application.

This suggests three other important observations: make sure you understand the criteria for promotion in your university, focus on contribution (not just activity), and write concisely.

Being clear about criteria – as the chapters of this book show promotion means different things in different places. Working out what counts within the discipline and in the university where you are applying starts with reading the written criteria. But these are often generalized and even where they are more specifically stated there is little sense of relative importance. Research into the published promotion criteria for universities in the Universitas 21 network by one of the editors of this volume (Jennifer Tatebe) also showed that there was significant variation across the network in promotion processes, application format, and required information with the format and requirements sometimes varying between departments/faculties *within* universities. Understanding these differing norms, weightings, and subtleties means attending briefing workshops (if they are offered), and identifying supportive colleagues who have *current* knowledge of the promotion process. I emphasize currency because criteria and interpretations evolve. Advice from someone with distant memory of the promotion process may not be that helpful or accurate.

Focus on contribution – an application for promotion differs from a curriculum vitae (CV). A CV sets out experiences and achievements. An application for promotion needs to explain the contribution or impact of your experiences and achievements. This poses some difficulties. A number of contributors to this volume have made reference to the need to "sell yourself." I understand the motivation for this advice but it can be misinterpreted. Perhaps I am interpreting the applications I have read through a New Zealand cultural lens that places a premium on humility but over-assertion of contribution is as damaging as under-representing it. Many of our contributions in the academy are collaborative and they should be noted as such. What promotion committees are looking for is to understand your contribution within that collaborative effort. Phrases such as "I shared ideas about," "I contributed to," "I was part of" are descriptions of role, not of contribution. Contribution is more active and specific. Compare, for example, "I was part of the teaching team for …" with

> *As part of the teaching team I took responsibility for the design and oversight of assessment. This meant drafting the tasks aligned to course outcomes and seeking comment from the rest of the team, revising the tasks, developing the assessment schedule and associated rubrics, posting the assessments for students, allocating the marking/grading amongst the team, chairing the moderation meeting and posting the grades. I also led the reflection on the assessment and as a consequence redesigned the requirements for the next iteration of the course.*

This captures the sense that you did not do everything (over-assertion) but it leaves the reader clear that you made a significant contribution to the team not only in an administrative sense but in a scholarly and academic way.

From a research perspective it is also important to explain your contribution in terms of the platform you are beginning to develop. It is not usually expected that in the early stages of an academic career that you will have a fully formed platform because you are likely to still be exploring different strands of research. But some sense of the way that your work is beginning to form around some key ideas and themes helps give the sense that your contribution is more than quantum (number of publications) and that it is about thoughtful development.

I have already noted the importance of emphasizing contribution and influence in your service contributions rather than simply recording what, without elaboration, may appear to be time filling on committees.

Write concisely – writing to the criteria helps with precision. If word limits are set then stick to them. Support claims with evidence incorporating the key evidence into the narrative and using appendices to provide further detail. As noted in the first section of this chapter citing convincing evidence to support claims about teaching is often challenging. The aforementioned research across Universitas 21 universities revealed a great deal of variety in the type of evidence used to support claims of teaching excellence. To avoid lengthy evidence-free descriptions of teaching look back at the examples offered by Jackie Cawkwell in her chapter, or consider organizing your response around the evidence categories developed by the Royal Academy of Engineering (Graham, 2016) – namely, a self-reflective narrative, a description of professional activities in teaching and learning (e.g., roles such as those described above in relation to assessment, annotated examples of course designs drawing attention to key teaching and

learning features, attendance at professional development courses in teaching and action arising from those courses), indirect
measures of student learning (e.g., changes in pass rates, reten-
tion rates, and grade distributions), direct measures of student
learning (e.g., pre- and post-assessments), and peer evaluation
and recognition (e.g., responses to observations and awards).

CONCLUSION

I salute the initiative in producing this publication. More than
anything, reading the chapters has reminded me of the unwit-
ting assumptions we make about promotion. The stories and
examples of variety and difference illustrate the complexity
of what is for those involved an important and emotional
process. The contributors have offered honest insights into
their personal and national experiences that will be read with
interest by early career academics and that should also be
read by promotion committees concerned with making fair
and equitable judgments about their colleagues.

Note

1. In this chapter I am viewing promotion through the lens of the
tenure track model rather than the open vacancy model (see the
Kivistö, Pekkola, and Pausits's chapter in this volume) although the
observations transfer, at least in part, between the two models.

REFERENCE

Graham, R. (2016). *Does teaching advance your academic
career?* Royal Academy of Engineering. Retrieved from
www.raeng.org.uk/evaluatingteaching

INDEX

Note: page numbers in italic and bold refers to figures and tables respectively & page numbers followed by 'n' refers to endnotes.